THE
ACTUALITY
OF THE
REALITY
OF THE
IMMATERIALITY

THE
ACTUALITY
OF THE
REALITY
OF THE
IMMATERIALITY

"A Theoretical Construct for Christian Psychiatry"

The Brain Is Not the Mind —
God Ain't Stupid and He Ain't Impractical

W. L. RYDER, M.D.

XULON PRESS

Xulon Press
2301 Lucien Way #415
Maitland, FL 32751
407.339.4217
www.xulonpress.com

Editorial Director: C. R. Brightwell, crb2646@yahoo.com

Front Cover Image by Erika Hollier, Graphics Artist/Designer

Book Design by Erika Hollier, Graphics Artist/Designer

Printed in the United States of America.

ISBN-13: 978-1-6312-9163-0

I am so grateful and thankful for the opportunity to work with Dr. Ryder in his psychiatric practice as mentor, co-worker and friend for 18 years. I was fortunate to work alongside him 10 of those years as he treated folks with mental illness and other various problems. He was a master at blending spiritual truths and biopsychosocial principals.

As a seminary graduate in psychology and counseling, I was especially interested in his multi-faceted approach in the psychology of conversion, involving challenging concepts which took time to process. However, I was fortunate to be working with him during his writing of this book and this, inevitably, allowed me to process the information with his feedback. Though challenging, Dr. Ryder's explanations always come back to the point of understanding crucial concepts. His writing style is very genuine and forthright, i.e, "sometimes you have to call a spade a spade". He is open, humble and humorous in sharing his own struggles towards growing in his faith in Christ, day-by-day and situation-by-situation. So sit back, take it in at your own pace and enjoy the ride moving forward in your own transformation in Christ Jesus.

I believe his goal was to promote deeper insights into our total humanity as spiritual beings, recognizing our need for Christ in our lives in practical day-to-day transformation, in order to manage life abundantly and to impact others to the grace and truth found only in Christ Jesus.

Terri Price, M.Div; LPC/S
Lake Charles, LA

* * * * * * * * * * * * * * * * *

I have often thought about my time working with Dr. Ryder. Honestly, in the beginning I wondered why this accomplished psychiatrist was still working, not off retired enjoying the wonderful life he had created for himself and his family. It became immediately evident that this was his life's calling — A calling from a place of true compassion, care, sincerity and spirituality. There in that moment, in that place, the patients experienced his greatest gift....healing, hope and faith.

Yolanda Johnson, LCSW
Baton Rouge, Louisiana

* * * * * * * * * * * * * * * * *

This book begins with questions and proceeds with conclusions tested and proven over a lifetime of practice. As a Christian who is also a psychiatrist, Dr. Ryder sought a way to integrate his practice with his Christian faith. In these pages, he presents that approach. While many others have attempted to do the same, Dr. Ryder writes as fellow struggler, not some wisened sage who has come down from the mountain to share his forgone and beyond question conclusions.

As his onetime pastor and longtime friend, I spent many sessions discussing with him his unique take on Christian psychiatry and psychology, I can thus highly recommend this book to those who are struggling with the age-old questions of human purpose, destiny, and the meaning of life from a Biblical and Christian perspective.

David Holder, D.Min.
Cornerstone Baptist Church
Texarkana, Arkansas

* * * * * * * * * * * * * * * * * *

My father had an abiding love for people. He had a special ability to convey how important it was for even a stranger to feel God's desire to save, His love for even the least lovable among us. I have had so many former patients, friends, and associates say to me how my father talked to them like no other person, much less a psychiatrist, and that he had taken so much time to explain things, spiritual or otherwise, to them personally regardless of any other concerns. He really didn't mind how much time it took, just as long as you left with a deeper understanding of how God left us a framework in His Word that transcends every other world view out there. That is what he meant when he said so colloquially, "God ain't stupid, and He ain't impractical." He was quick to point out whenever any of his children acted otherwise, but he left it up to us to discover our own mistakes and come to our own corrective actions, eventually and hopefully, always willing to share his perspective and wisdom gleaned from scripture and experience. He taught me how satisfying it was to use medicine as an occasion to teach others eternal truths, first by making them "weller," as he was wont to say, never so rash to claim he could cure anyone. This would so often segue way into a natural discussion of how

God provides for not only our physical but also our mental and spiritual health. He lived to see others glimpse God's seed take root in their lives and encourage them to see it grow to fruition in whatever soil they had, unafraid to add whatever he could to help them along. He embodied God's admonition to His disciples to feed His sheep and spread His Word, using the principles of psychiatry and psychoanalysis to upend the Humanists' secular and bankrupt philosophy.

Garrett B Ryder, MD
Medical Director
Gulf Coast Psychiatry

* * * * * * * * * * * * * * * * * *

Like the blind man whose eyes were opened, when Lew Ryder encountered the Lord, his eyes and his heart were forever changed. I am a lifelong witness of his steadfast and passionate devotion to God. Hear him now and fall in love with Jesus as he did.

Sharon Davis, RN
Baton Rouge, La

* * * * * * * * * * * * * * * * * *

I had the privilege of working with Dr. Ryder for over 20 years in mental health. He was the medical director of the company that I owned. It didn't take long for me to see his love for helping people who were struggling with mental disorders. It was a privilege to be able to sit with him after work hours were over and just talk about particular cases and ask questions I had in helping others through Christian counseling.

Dr. Ryder spent a lot of time talking about the difference between the brain and the mind. We also spent a lot of time talking about how spiritual issues affected mental health.

Dr. Ryder allowed me to be a part of the genesis of this book. It was an honor for me to be able to read some of the early drafts and to see how he was connecting the spiritual with the emotional and mental. Dr. Ryder was not just a psychiatrist who was a Christian, but he was a Christian who used not only the academic studies of psychiatry, but also used spiritual principles to help people struggling with mental health.

I hope this book can help others improve their ability to use spiritual principles to affect mental health.

Ronnie Burke, B.A. (Education), M.R.E., Dr. of Bible Theology
Sulphur, Louisiana.

* * * * * * * * * * * * * * * * * *

As a third-generation psychiatrist, I had accepted the statistical eventuality that I would someday see patients treated by my father and potentially my grandfather. Imagine my surprise, then, when this eventuality came to be a reality while I was in residency in a state neither man had ever practiced in. A patient and their family member came into my clinic and stated that they were amazed and excited at the coincidence of seeing another "Dr. Ryder" who was also a psychiatrist. You see, they explained, the last "Dr. Ryder" was a Christian psychiatrist back in the 1970s who was able to provide compassionate care the likes of which they had not experienced since then. There were many times they suffered from active symptoms as well as the devastating impact of the disorder, even while "in remission." They told me how, remembering the talks with my grandfather in his office about their faith, they found a peace that medicine could not bring them despite decades of advancement. This poignant moment in my training as a new psychiatrist taught me that faith can help reach patients in ways modern medicine never could. My grandfather had recently passed into eternal life, but I could almost hear his laughter echoing that familiar, "God ain't stupid, and He ain't impractical!" He wrote this book to teach precisely this lesson, hoping that the words contained herein could help us to achieve more for our patients.

Zachary Ryder, MD
Medical Director
Access Serenity of Louisiana
Lake Charles, LA

* * * * * * * * * * * * * * * * * *

From his multi-faceted life experiences as entrepreneur, soldier, husband, father, grandfather, healer, and above all, humane and spiritual person, Dr. Ryder developed a unique and valuable perspective as both a psychiatrist and an individual of consequence, optimism, and hope, which he shares in this book. Having known him was a privilege and a pleasure, when I worked with him in his later years. It was a great pleasure to watch him display his boundless kindness and caring as he interacted with everyone he encountered, both colleagues and patients alike. He cared about everyone, and most could sense that. Our work was with the most seriously mentally ill, who needed not only his knowledge and skill, but also that caring from him and from all of us on the team. Although he's gone now, his spirit remains with all who knew him, and so does his message (excerpted in part here from "A Fallen Limb") to those who follow: "Grieve not for me. Remember the best times, the laughter, the song. The good life I lived while I was strong. Continue my heritage, I'm counting on you. Keep smiling and surely the sun will shine through...." The light from the "sun" of his perspective and caring will be evident to readers, and will be something to carry with you, and to carry on. As he was a person whom one remembered and appreciated, his contributions in this book will also be remembered and appreciated. An unforgettable person and a memorable book. Take the time to read and absorb his message. I don't think you'll regret it.

Foley L. Nash, LPC-S, LMFT-BAS
Director of Clinical Services–Behavioral Health
Aetna Better Health of Louisiana

This book is an opportunity for you to enrich your life by meeting Dr. Lewis Ryder, a unique Christian Psychiatrist who very thoughtfully made his own path during his 90 years, practicing until his passing in 2017. He was a father of 9 children, an entrepreneur, and an MD with a singular psychiatric practice that ministered effectively to all who came under his care. In his book, which friends and patients asked him to write, Dr. Ryder focuses on the truths about each of us. You can trust that he has researched every principle and brought to bear his long experience to uncover the core needs of every person.

Take to heart what you read here and draw comfort from this very wise counselor who cared deeply about the most important questions each of us has about our lives and the meaning of our lives.

Suzanne Gann
Lawrenceville, GA

* * * * * * * * * * * * * * * * *

I had the privilege of working with Dr. Ryder for 3 years. The meaningful impact of having known him is not something I can easily communicate, but the Lord knows in full.

Dr. Ryder was zealous about truth. He had a strong distaste for the artificial or shallow. He never related to his patients as sets of behaviors or objects upon which to perform techniques, but related to the human soul beneath even the most severe state of mental illness. It was an authenticity that people could sense at a gut level, no matter their mental status, and I witnessed the way that people responded to that. He worked to help patients come more nearly to reality, particularly by pointing out the reality of those things that are unseen, which so often motivate our behavior. Many times in conversation he would ask me, "Now why did you choose that particular word?" (as opposed to another with the same meaning, but the slightest difference in connotation.) In all of our subtle choice of words, he knew the choices themselves communicated something.

He worked fervently until the very end of his life to glorify God and to build up those who were deeply suffering. Because of that fire he had in him, no amount of time was ever too long with a patient (or a co-worker for that matter). He seemed to run the race without weariness.

What a treasure to have his "voice" preserved in writing. I think what makes this approach to therapy stand alone among others is that it is the only one that fully speaks to our human circumstances—that we live in the midst of the reality of death. Yet we have a great hope which Dr. Ryder displayed and constantly pointed others toward throughout his life's work. I am personally so very thankful for this man who truly was in an instrument of grace in my own life.

Aimee Keith, Behavioral Health Case Manager
Lake Charles, LA

* * * * * * * * * * * * * * * * * *

Dr. Ryder's book offers both a necessary analysis and perspective of what the world needs today to make some sense of what is going on all around each and every one of us. His research and study has produced a gift easily understandable for every age. With his knowledge of today's needs, problems and solutions, his approach is balanced and practical.

Karen Douglass, Secretary
Lake Charles, La

TABLE OF CONTENTS

Case Studies:

Understanding EGP with Specific Persons and Their Issues

DEDICATION

Dedicated to the preservation of my Christian heritage, instilled in me by the grace of God through my parents. Eternal thanks and love to all who assisted me in compiling and completing this fruitful labor, including my many colleagues, all my patients, my entire beloved family and friends who find we all are "swimming in the same stuff" while walking this earth until we get to heaven.

See you there!

THE BRAIN IS NOT THE MIND

W hen I was about five years old, I was lying on my front porch relaxing and enjoying a beautiful spring day. As I watched the sky, the white puffy clouds formed a six-horse stage-coach with all the details. Of course, I knew it was not real because if I looked away it would not be the same when I looked back. I remember thinking, "That is interesting. How does that happen?" Then I said to myself, "It happened because I was thinking it. How did my thoughts become the picture I saw in the clouds?" I have been chasing that question ever since.

I have come a long way in understanding some of the significance of what thoughts are, where they come from, and why we have them. Finally, I came to this important, critical and essential realization:

**The brain is not the mind—
HOWEVER,
The mind is a function of the brain.**

The mind is where we ask questions and seek answers. So, that led me on a quest to understand more of what the mind does and in the process I began to ask these age-old questions:

What difference does my life make, if any?
Where did I come from?
What am I doing here?
Where am I going? If anywhere?
And, what difference does it make, anyhow?

Eventually as an adult, I walked down the aisle of a church where the pastor stated, "Folks, I do not know it all and do not have all the answers, but I will tell you what I believe."

That pastor's honest and frank statement finally did it for me! Jesus became not only my Savior but the Lord of my life! I understood and decided to believe that He was the only One who could give me the answers to life and when we refer to eternal life. "I have come that they might have life, and have *it* more abundantly," Jesus said in John 10:10 (NKJV). To me that meant if I surrender to the truth that God gives in Christ then I will be alright no matter what the circumstances. I can then live a life with purpose here on the earth, and when I die, I am going to be secure because Jesus has overcome death. I am going to be secure in spite of anything and everything the world throws at me. I have a reason and purpose to live and I can die without fear, looking forward to eternal life with Christ.

THE AWAKENING

For more than three decades of study and professional practice, I have worked as a Christian psychiatrist to integrate biblical principles into the vital task of helping people heal both physically and emotionally. For twenty-five years before that, I wandered in a spiritual wilderness, attempting to provide healing for people through the usual approaches of secular counseling. I, like so many others, helped many hurting people. Nonetheless, I also have vivid memories of those I was not able to help fully. The psycho-dynamic principles guiding me at that time left out the key dimension of the human personality. Namely, that:

**We are made in the image of God.
Therefore, only God, Who is all-power,
can heal the mind's diseases.**

Permit me to expand upon that for you. The body is not what is made in His image because God doesn't have a body. God said, "I am Spirit." Then He said, "Those who worship Me must worship Me in Spirit and in truth" (John 4:24 KJV). Since this biblical passage is an imperative, a commandment, if we desire to worship God, it behooves us to understand the words of the instruction in order to more nearly be able to *do* or *perform* them. This is a first purpose of this book. We must remember, "God ain't stupid and He ain't impractical," so there must be a way to do what He commands. Only God has the power to empower and heal someone physically and/or psycho-spiritually.[1] He is the only One Who can *empower* us to participate to a point of healing the soul's dis-eases. "God has not given us a Spirit of fear but of power, and of love, and of a **sound mind**" (2 Timothy 1:7 NKJV emphasis added). You may ask, "How does that work? Why do we (I) have so much trouble?" Consistent with a first order of purpose of this book, we will talk about how that works and what interferes with it.

---

[1] Later in this book, I will differentiate between organic mental illness or brain disease and purely emotional, or psychological, or neurotic illnesses. Nothing about schizophrenia, bipolar, autism, or ADHD for instance primarily involves choice or an act of will. Each is a condition, like a brain tumor or stroke that affects the function of the brain called the mind. Chemical imbalance of the brain resulting in mental symptoms, when given appropriate chemicals (molecules) the brain's electro-chemical activity fires better and the mind functions better and there are fewer symptoms but that person not cured yet, which that qualitative element of His nature -- that *Elohim* God Power element -- could do, but physical medicine can only improve, help maintain, OR make better. In general, however, such treatment is still to be valued and seen as the blessing from God that it is, and used to help humans with mental, emotional, or psychiatric problems. As far as I am concerned, I believe God even today still does instantaneous miracles, but His EGP (*Elohim* God Power) seems to be more frequently available to us humans where there has been personal choice involved WITH HIM in the problem. I'm talking primarily about neuroses, purely psychological, in contrast to purely organic or physical conditions. Remember: every neurotic symptom is a direct expression of the sin nature in that it (the symptom) is a maladaptive effort–an effort, but one that never works–to deny or distort the truth that I have no power! Coming to terms with that reality before and in relationship with God (Who is all that is Power, and all Love that is Love), a person can be okay even though everything here now ain't okay, even unto death, the fear of which underlies all neurotic behavior. (Hebrews 2:15)

It's not as though I had not been exposed to spiritual truth early in life. In fact, my family was Christian and God's grace saved me at nine. When I heard both the Baptists and Catholics say they had *THE* answer, and also the Methodists, Presbyterians, Episcopalians, and Lutherans claim it, too, I was not so much confused as I just knew something was surely amiss. In truth, they all do have *the* answer, Jesus Christ, but He's not Who or what they seem to focus on.

I discovered early in life that being saved and influenced by Jesus' teachings did not keep me from negative attitudes and actions that readily served my sin nature's resistance to Christian growth and making right decisions. Somewhat like Job, without relinquishing my faith, I was argumentative with God's Word (the Scriptures), resisting a complete commitment to living the Christian life. This ambivalence persisted throughout high school, service in World War II, undergraduate and medical school studies, eight years of general medical practice, three years of psychiatric residency, and four years of further training in psychoanalysis. Consequently, during those years I "wandered in the wilderness."

Spiritual Wounding in a Christian College

A significant spiritual wounding in college contributed to my wanderings by compounding the doubts I already had because of unanswered questions. When discussing God's omnipotence ("all power belongs to God" according to Psalm 62:11), my renowned Bible professor repeatedly disallowed my question because of his misinterpretation as my inherent doubting, *"If* God is omnipotent...." and interrupted me saying, "You mean '*Since* God is omnipotent...'"

I had not intended my question to be argumentative or expressing any unbelieving doubt in God's Power, but this professor immediately assumed that to be the case. It was a genuine, *seeking inquiry about* and *towards* God! My heartfelt need was to have some sense of rational, intellectual explanation about the mind-boggling Omnipotence of God because I hoped to gain further Spiritual insight (i.e., Revelation [2], though I didn't fully understand it would be that at that time.)

My desire was to develop a *reasonable* faith that could stand firm and be built upon. My professor, a highly regarded Christian Bible scholar, missed that I was genuinely seeking God. Instead, he assumed I was trying to argue with him. Proverbs 8:17 promises, "...those who seek me [God] diligently will find me" (NKJV). Scripture also promises, "I did not say to the seed of Jacob, 'Seek Me in vain,'" (Isaiah 45:19 NKJV), and, "And you will seek Me and find Me, when you search for Me with all your heart" (Jeremiah 29:13 NKJV).

After several failed attempts to pose this question, in disappointed frustration I left the class. My feeling attitude was that if *this* Christian's faith was so defensively fragile as to not be able to discern genuine inquiry (in contrast to accusatory repudiation),

---

[2] The theological concept of Revelation is much more than what is usually understood by usual exposure to Revelation. We will discuss further in the book the significance of the meaning of this doctrine.

then obviously my reluctant skepticism about Christianity had been right all along! The adversary (Satan) had won a battle (not the war!). My soul was left pleading for *something more* than what I was experiencing at a Christian college or, for that matter, for me at that time from any other source of Christian inquiry including, and perhaps especially so, the Church.

This exposure came at that most vulnerable time of any young person's bio-psycho-socio-spiritual development, the ages between the late teens and late twenties. Right when every youth is in the throes of trying to clarify and differentiate the foundational pillars upon which he/she can build his/her own sense of personal identity. Consciously or unconsciously, inherent in this struggle are the universally human questions:

- Where did I come from, if anywhere?
- What am I doing here, if anything?
- Where am I going, if anywhere? And what difference does it make, if any?

Underlying all this intellectually and emotionally turbulent effort is an experiential *sense of need for security*. It seems, for most, this effort turns out to last a lifetime.

A General Practitioner's Experience of Life

My academic background includes the usual four years of undergraduate studies, four years of medical school, followed by a one-year internship. At that point, I had a family and could not then afford to enter the specialty of psychiatry, as I had previously planned. Instead, I opened a general practice of medicine and surgery. For eight years I developed a holistic approach in treating my patients as they experienced the fears, doubts, and pain of parents and children who were being treated for "strep" throat, measles, polio, pneumonia, or serious physical trauma. I guided girls and women through prenatal care, delivering their wonderfully healthy, sometimes not-so-healthy, and, yes, even sometimes deformed or dead babies. In all of this, I was exposed to humanness, life, and *its most common attendant experience—**death**.*[3]

In 1962, I was fortunate enough to be awarded a National Institute of Mental Health (NIMH) grant to complete what I had intended to do before I went to undergraduate school, to become a psychoanalyst. Three years of residency in general psychiatry were followed by four years of formal, academic course work in the theory and practice of psychoanalysis, including four years of personal analysis, and one year of supervision of an assigned analytical case. It took this long for me to recognize (by the grace of God) that although psychoanalysis as a method has much validity, please understand it is not a panacea. It is not for everyone and, for various reasons, is not appropriate for the majority of patients. In fact, for many people in acute or severe distress, it is even contra-indicated and not an option. This is not to say I would trade my training for any other. I am convinced the Lord "raised me up in the way to go" with the purpose of being

---

[3] Another actual point of consideration has to include **death and its meaning and how that relates to "something more"** searched for and alluded to throughout this book as an underlying thread involved in the psychology of conversion throughout life which, obviously, cannot be avoided by anyone.

able to discern a secular vs. a Biblically Christian orientation and the differences it can make.

Eventually, I decided not to continue with psychoanalytic training as I came to realize that psychoanalysis did not answer those probing questions that plagued me. As I studied and understood more about what and where this training was coming from and what it was about, the less meaningful it became for me. Even though I was not fully engaged in a relationship with God, I knew I could not truly holistically approach treatment of my patients without including God in the equation. None of the other approaches included anything spiritual. They did not include Christ therefore they did not give hope!

Without God I found I had nothing but humanistic orientation, naturalistic orientation, and evolutionism which has no hope and gives no purpose. Camus, the humanistic philosopher, said: "There's not but really one question for human beings and that is, shall I commit suicide now or later?" So, I began asking,

What kind of philosophy is that?
What kind of worldview is that?
What kind of hope is that?

A Sunday Morning Epiphany

Vainly having searched diligently for that blessing of *"something more"* through the cross-discipline intellectual studies of philosophy, medicine, psychiatry and psychoanalysis, varied successful entrepreneurial business activities, and even successful politics, the prayers of my Godly Roman Catholic wife were answered. The Lord loved her and me enough to knock me to my knees, and He hit me right where He knew it would be most effective, i.e., in my prideful independence and my pocketbook.

This elicited from me a brilliant question: "Lord, are you trying to tell me something?"

God's answer was, "Yes, stupid! To be used [by Me] requires learning to *remember Who's Who!*"

Though I only rarely attended church, primarily for my kids' and wife's sakes, on this particular Easter Sunday morning I pleasantly surprised the family by volunteering to go to church with them. By the time we got all nine children into our van and we were about halfway there, I realized it was too late to make the Mass at "their" church and said so. Having inquired about the possibility before, the children almost in unison suggested, "Well, let's go to your church for the first time, Daddy." (My wife had never been *against* the idea.)

Without even having considered it previously that morning and almost simultaneously thinking it was a good idea, I realized we were right then at the entrance to a large Baptist church. I could see the parking lot was packed full, overflowing with cars lined up even onto the sidewalk grass next to the street from the city block, corner to corner. Almost spilling the kids, I suddenly slowed and turned sharply into the lot thinking, "I'll never find a parking space!"

Unbelievably (miraculously), as I straightened the car up in the driveway, there immediately in front of me was a single, sole, open parking spot on the end of the row I was on. We hurried into the church and were ushered upstairs into a sort of side cubby of the balcony. Our family of two parents and nine children filled one entire pew in the balcony.

At that particular time, an interim pastor was serving the church. He (like the college professor) was another scholarly, eminent Christian who was the president of a large seminary. I now know that for years God had been preparing my *spirit, soul, and body* to hear *such a man* say, while making a theologically-oriented doctrinal point, "...I probably don't know everything about all this, but I can tell you what I've come to believe."

I heard him say between the lines, "I *could* be wrong." Yet his confidently transparent and reasoned faith asserted, "But I believe...."

My years of accumulated resistances to Christian faith began to melt away. My psycho-spiritual tumblers all suddenly began to fall into place as the Holy Spirit instantly liberated me.

I went forward with tears streaming down my face to acknowledge and surrender to Jesus Christ, not only as my Savior, which I had already DONE, but now I surrendered to Christ as the *Lord of my life.*

Over the next few months, my wife and all nine children, each on his or her own, surrendered to Jesus Christ and entered into a personal relationship with Him. I began an intensive study into what the Bible has to say about the human personality, about why we experience so much pain and struggle so hard for significance. I learned God's truth about why we so greatly fear death and will try almost anything to escape it. The "something more" that I was searching for was a theological/psychological construct that took into account absolute Truth as presented in Scriptures.[4] It provided a Biblical perspective on the human condition and the human personality, *including an understandable psychology of conversion.*

This book presents the results of that search as tested over more than forty years of counseling both believers and nonbelievers who, in their lives, have experienced the worst kinds of emotional trauma and, therefore, exhibited the most extreme maladaptive behaviors the world of counseling has to offer.

The Need for Truth and Surviving Death

Early on in my understanding and the further I went into my psychiatric/psychoanalytic training, the more I realized the "this-worldliness" and self-centeredness of the human personality in its focus on the *survival* of "self." After a particular three-day seminar, I challenged the internationally eminent professor lecturing that he seemed to be saying that survival ultimately was

---

[4] The thrust of my practice from the 1970's has been to correlate the valid psychological principles with the Biblical principles. I want the reader to note, however, that the psychological principles gain their validity by the fact of first having been presented from Scripture, not vice versa. And, if there seems to be a contradiction, I choose to go obediently with God Almighty.

the only thing that had any meaning. After a brief thoughtful moment, he agreed. Surprisingly, the shallowness of such a philosophy of life, *and its inherent worldview,* suddenly crystallized in my mind. Here's a singular and primary truth which I presented to him:

If there is nothing worth dying for, how can there be anything worth living for?

If there is no cause, no absolute principle of moral truth, or even ethical reality worth dying for, then the struggles of everyday life can hardly be worth the living.

The credo of existential philosophy and psychology is its emphasis on "present experience" ***as the only truth or reality.*** This leaves us empty of any other source of certain, eternal or absolute, Truth and/or the ***Promise of Security*** beyond our own "selves." The extant alternative "source" is the other like-limited and vulnerable "existing selves" in our immediate environment. To *begin* to comprehend the hopelessness inherent in such a credo, a person must begin to think about and realize that "one's personhood's" *immediate environment* is ultimately all physical materiality. This *environment* that "you" and "I" exist and move about in is **physical.** This "personal space," the context in which "you" and "I" exist is *physical* (i.e., our bodies). "We" exist in the context of molecules, atoms, and subatomic particles, the configuration of which we call a "body" having measurable mass and weight.

This physical, measurable weight and mass configuration we call our body exists and moves about in another "immediate, but separate environment," most of which we can't see, but is experienced demonstrably by the commonly known phenomenon which we call "atmospheric pressure." This phenomenon expresses the reality of the unseen weighted mass in the "empty" space of our immediate external environment. This phenomenon results from the measured action of God's natural law of gravity pulling all the atoms and molecules in "empty space" toward earth. The atmospheric pressure gets less as the distance from the earth grows, not only because the number of atoms and molecules decrease, but because the pull of gravity has less influence on them.

So, existential and other humanistic, materialistic philosophy and psychology offer no source of Truth or Promise of Security to humans other than man's "self" *in* his *most immediate* environment, which is his body. If we think about this closely, honestly, and accurately, all of which means truthfully and realistically, we must conclude that the body is only physical in that it is comprised of subatomic particles, atoms, and molecules. This is the same "stuff" of which a rock, oil, wood, air, or the book you're holding consists.

While constituted of the identical stuff of which the whole universe is made, the human body is configured not into rock, oil, air, or wood but into what we call amino acids, polypeptides, and proteins — the building blocks of tissue – and that tissue is configured into organs and organs into the organ system we call the body. So when you see your hand holding this book, you can ask yourself, "If the two are made up of the same stuff and in one hundred years whatever was left could be filtered out and no one could differentiate which was which, what is the difference right now?"

So, what *is the singularly primary* difference between your hand and the book I have personally wondered and responded to? Don't be surprised if it took you a moment because most people don't give much thought to such considerations or see any reason to. But, yes, the hand has life in it and the book does not! It is dead; it has no life in it! Like the body when the "life" leaves this atomic, molecular, physical substance, it – the substance — is dead! Well, that's nice, but what *is* life? Where did life come from and what's the big deal anyhow? What difference does it make, if any?

Another point of consideration our reasoning intuitively seeks an intellectually satisfying answer to is, "What is the mind?" Let me state unequivocally, "<u>The brain is not the mind!</u>" The mind, however, is a function of the brain, **but only as long as the "I" of "me" is in this body!** I will discuss later in this book how the spirit informs the mind.

Responding to these puzzling, enigmatic questions is one of the main themes of this book. We will elaborate and present what seem to be very reasonable, intelligent conclusions to the glory of God, and for the bio-psycho-socio-spiritual benefit (i.e., peace, comfort, and joy—or eternal health) of those who apply its pragmatic, eternal practicality.

So what I am trying to stir into your intelligent awareness is:

The reality or truth is that no intelligent, discerning, and free-will person (self) would even claim that anything in human history or experience holds out any promise whatsoever for man's Security to reside in humankind or the environment that humans have experienced.

A Note about the Nature of Humanism

It will be useful here to be unequivocally clear about the nature of Humanism and the bases of its principles and worldview. On two separate occasions, it has been judged by the Supreme Court to be a religion. This is of no small importance when we consider the impact of its influence on Western Culture since 1933 when the first Humanist Manifesto was written. This influence has been especially felt through the school system.

First and foremost, it must be understood that it is unapologetically and aggressively atheistic. Humanism's atheistic intellectual elitism imposes an attitude of their having the right and moral duty to inform the proletariat (regular folks) what is best for them and the intellectually elite will provide the way. Their goals will be accomplished through "education and public proclamation" — through teaching methods in schools, the social sciences, literature, movies, music, news print, social mores and moral values – and any other available avenue — to remove even the consideration of the notion of reasonableness to the possibility of the actuality of the reality of immateriality (such as the spirit world and a creator God). "Humanism begins with nature, not God." Their goal is not the separation of church and state. Rather, it is the separation of God from the socio-politico-cultural landscape, and even more so, the very concept of God from the awareness of human cognition!

There is no hope without God!
Without hope, what have I got?

Two of their main tenets that flavor all the others are: (1) We begin with nature not God and (2) Since there is no Deity to save mankind, man must save himself. This results in people worshipping at the altar of science. This means man can only deal with, or even intellectually pursue, physical materiality — in other words, the things of this world (i.e., the universe). As all materialists do, they deny and/or refute the reality of anything that can't be weighed and measured. This limits the scope of their knowledge and understanding.

God says their wisdom — the very cornerstone of their prideful, narcissistic worldview — is therefore of naught because "The fear of the Lord is the beginning of wisdom" (Psalm 111:10). They have no fear of the Lord, therefore, do not even have the *beginning* of **wisdom**. We must remember, "The things of God are foolishness to natural (unregenerate) (materialist) man. Natural man does not understand, and he **cannot** understand

because they are **spiritually** discerned" (1 Corinthians 2:14 NIV emphasis mine).

Can Psychology Be a Substitute for God's Word?

Since stepping out of psychoanalytic training and changing the direction of my life, my studies and counseling experience have brought me full circle from attempting to substitute psychology for religion back to the Bible as God's Word, the ultimate and only *real* Truth. The condition of the world, our country, its changing culture, and the effects on society — and *especially on the church* — have forced me to address a need I see in counseling. Increasing numbers of people are coming in with the pain and suffering of family, work, and other interpersonal relationships. This also includes an increasing percentage — not just an increase in numbers — of church-going Christians who are unsure of their religion's "truth."

Increasingly, patients have asked that I put into book form what I have helped them come to understand in resolving their problems. Clergymen, both patients and non-patients, have asked and encouraged me as well to write down my insights into human personality gleaned from Scripture and my clinical practice.

Most of all, however, it has been the continued prodding by the Holy Spirit, Who has encouraged me to undertake this difficult task. Only God knows what an unlikely candidate I am to be speaking to others about Him, not only because of my own sinfulness, but also because of the dyslexia from which He has allowed me to suffer. The event that finally pushed me past all resistance, though, was the Board of Trustees of my own American Psychiatric Association insisting an official position that it would be "unethical" for a practitioner to say he was practicing "Christian Psychiatry" because "there is no such thing." Since I have been practicing this discipline for more than four decades, it seems essential to make clear that there *are* elements of a definitive Christian psychiatry, one founded and elaborated upon from Biblical principles and inspiration.

Unfortunately, the board was somewhat right in that there exists no statement of a general theory or theoretical construct for a biblically-based, Christian psychiatric practice. Several people have produced informative and useful books on counseling, psychotherapy, and even psychiatry emphasizing Scripture and its application. I thank God for these authors and books. I and many others have found them helpful. However, their goals and aims have not necessarily been the same as those being addressed here. So, in the next chapter, I will lay down some foundational principles for understanding and applying a Christian Counseling Theory.[5]

---

[5] Comment on Dr. Ryder's Unique Style: My father called upon me to assist him at times with the writing and editing of this book. He struggled much with the given task because, despite his high view of God, the importance of obedience and the gifts of a wealth of education, intellect, vocabulary, insight, wisdom, professional expertise and dyslexia, to name but a few, he never wanted to shame the name of the Lord. He wanted to write a worthy book. His body failed him before completion, as it died a short time ago.

So, I am left to provide a bit of clarity regarding his very unique and expert style of delivery the importance of each subject and its language. He was generally the same whether the audience was family, friends, or patients; however, poignancy ruled explicitly when wisdom was called for. He was fun and professional to the core, never missing the serious beat. Dad's efforts in reducing to writing a semblance of what real talk therapy was like yielded the creation of his own vocabulary. Not really his own dictionary, but for him and, as it turns out, for all of us including his patients, it was very important to emphasize the meaning of words when and how they are used. If a person is not used to hearing him clarify that it's always best to say what you mean and mean what you say, it just might make

Insights for You to Know and Apply

➢ *We are made in the image of God; therefore, only God has the power to heal the MIND's (soul's) dis-eases.*

➢ *If there is nothing worth dying for, how can there be anything worth living for? If there is no cause, no absolute principle of moral truth, or even ethical reality worth dying for, then the struggles of everyday life can hardly be worth the living.*

➢ *The reality is that no intelligent, discerning, and free-will person (self) would have the power to claim anything in*

---

conversational life more difficult. However, on the other hand, when absorbed, it made life significantly more alive! Also, he had a tendency to capitalize a lot! He often capitalizes the first letter of certain words and other times the entire word gets the same treatment with additional bold or italicized highlighting. Then, of course, is to enjoy his lengthy sentence structure. Please do not allow any of this to detract or distract, but read through it with pleasure You will find, then, many things you never wanted to miss anyway.

His style is not for naught, either. When speaking with someone it's easier to repeat a meaningful word to emphasize what may be casually overlooked in daily affairs and which very well may not yet be realized as what's negatively or positively impacting someone. Additionally, "biblically Christian" is another unique phrase my father often used, though sparingly yet appropriately so but, most often, only within the context of the office setting. The phrase can be confusing, of course, without knowing his intent. To simplify that intent, let me just say that it aligns no differently with what ministers preach when challenging hearers to read and apply the Scriptures. However, my father was not the preacher, he was the doctor. When any of us find ourselves struggling to manage life's demands, our emotions and even our limitations can dim what we expect of our selves, Christian or not. So, as a psychotherapist using biblical principles to help his patients – not to save them, as that is Christ's work – my father would begin effectively using this phrase when uncovering patients' respective issues to pinpoint and punctuate, again and again until it "sunk in," how Bible teachings (or, maybe with non-believers, the essence of them) might apply and then be used to better understand "how we tick the way we do, and why we have so much trouble."

So, this book should not be read in any other way than if you knew the man himself and the beauty of his verbiage. Were you to ask those who did enjoy time spent with one of God's best, they would say to not worry about writing style, but to just please take the delicious truth of the messenger and you will experience greater peace, comfort and joy.

As Winston Churchill famously stated, "Men occasionally stumble over the truth, but most of them pick themselves up and hurry off as if nothing ever happened."

human history or experience that holds out any promise whatsoever for man's Security.

➢ *God alone is omnipotent; all power belongs to God.*

➢ *Materiality, humanity, and the environment offer no promise of <u>Security</u> for the self.*

➢ *Humanism denies God therefore it is one of the main tools of the devil in our times.*

HOW DOES GOD'S DESIGN OF PERSONALITY THEORY AFFECT OUR AWARENESS OF WHO WE ARE?

The Lord was working on me and in my life all that time I was searching for answers. I was in the throes of doubt with serious questions about what to do with my life when all my studies still left me without the answers I so desperately needed.

Then I attended a three-day symposium conducted by a brilliant training analyst who had written a book on the meaning of despair. After listening to him, I could not take it any longer.

Finally, I stood up and with much respect, I interrupted him and said, "It seems what you are saying is that survival is the only thing that really matters."

He looked at me, thought for a moment, and said that was a fair assessment of what he was presenting.

"So, if there is nothing worth dying for," I asked pointedly, "how can there be anything worth living for?"

Dead silence permeated the auditorium full of experts. I sat down. Instead of even trying to answer my question, he just went on presenting his agenda. It was at that point I concluded to myself, I am done with this. I have got to go in some other direction. This does not give me the answers that I have been looking for, but I know they are out there somewhere. After contemplating everything throughout the night, I went to my analytic session the next day, spoke with my advisor, and withdrew from my psychoanalytical training.

❧

The process of psychoanalysis taught me much about human personality and about psychology, but it did not give me the answers about the truth and reality I was searching for.

❧

God Is Not Stupid and He Is Not Impractical

My wife, nine kids, and I moved from Atlanta to Shreveport. It was Easter Sunday and we decided to gather all the kids and go to church together. We were running very late and the church we chose had cars all over the place but we finally found a parking place and quickly walked into the church. The service had already started and we occupied an entire pew in a nook in the balcony. It turns out the interim preacher was Dr. Landrum Leavell, the President of New Orleans Baptist Seminary.

He said, "Folks, I do not have all the answers, but I can tell you what I believe with all my heart."

Then he stated his beliefs with conviction in a very clear, concise form. I could hardly believe what I was hearing. In a matter of minutes, this one man seemed to know exactly what I needed to hear. It was like God sent us there and sent this man to minister just to me!

The tears just poured out of my eyes! I had such relief! I could not wait for the invitation to go to the altar! God had answered my questions. That was the day I received Jesus not only as my Savior, but as my Lord as well. I surrendered everything in my life to Him. I took what He said in the Bible as truth whether it made sense to me at the time or whether I could figure it out or not. The truth and reality I had been searching for were available through God's Word.

I began to teach in Sunday School and to lead Bible studies which prompted me to dig deeper and deeper into the Scriptures. My hunger for truth and reality was being satisfied as I learned more and more about God and His definition of life. One Sunday I did a study in Isaiah. Present was a young fellow in medical school who seemed particularly interested in what I was teaching.

He came to me after class and asked, "Dr. Ryder, would you talk to my medical class about the psychology of conversion?"

Without thinking twice, I agreed to do it. It did not dawn on me until later where this study was going to take me. When I began to work on helping this medical class understand the psychology of conversion, I became familiar with an aspect of God's truth I had not yet uncovered. It revolved around the fact that we are made up of spirit, soul, and body (Refer to diagram D1 on page 4).

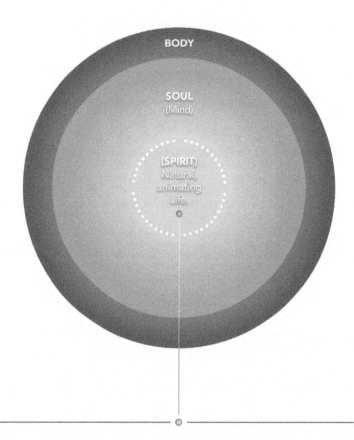

We must remember all three components are dead to God since the Fall.
[The capital "S" differentiates between the saved "born again" Spirit and the lost little "s," dead to God in trespass, and doesn't seem to designate the significance of the difference.] All the examples used in this book try to depict the devastatingly stark difference from saved to lost.

Every school of education I had studied had a theory of personality. I was discovering God did, too. However, God does not deal in just theory, He deals in truth and reality. He states His design for "theory" on personality very clearly in 1 Thessalonians 5:23 and Hebrews 4:1. The Apostle Paul wrote the words of his prayer for Christians in 1 Thessalonians 5:23 saying, "I pray God your whole spirit and soul and body be preserved blameless unto the coming of our Lord Jesus Christ" (KJV). Paul names these same three components again in Hebrews 4:12 where he says, "For the word of God is quick, and powerful, and sharper than any two-edged sword, piercing even to the dividing asunder of soul and spirit, and of the joints and marrow, and is a discerner of the thoughts and intents of the heart" (KJV) (Refer to diagram D2 on page 6).

○ Where the operation of the mental functions of:

Intelligence, Judgement, Will, Emotion, Intuition

take place

BODY

◎ SOUL

Greek word from which
we get our English word psyche
or psychology or MIND (mental activity)

"s"pirit

Greek meaning unreborn,
dead to God since the fall,
unregenerated, little "I" -
"I"ife and little "s" - "s"pirit
to designate merely
natural man.

Intelligence, Judgement, Will, Emotion, Intuition

1 THESS. 5:23

- and the very God of peace sanctify you wholly; and I
pray your whole spirit and soul and body be preserved
blameless unto the coming of our Lord Jesus Christ.

HEB. 4:12

- for the word of God is quick, and powerful, and sharper than any two-edged sword,
piercing even to the dividing asunder of soul and spirit, and of the joints and marrow,
and is a discerner of the thoughts and intents of the heart.

6

Scripture reveals that a person has three facets in his/her personality structure—*body, soul, and spirit.* This is the reality of who we are and how we "think." Can I believe and accept this truth? Of course, because I can assure you: *God is not stupid and He is not impractical.*

It became obvious to me that in order to be the kind of physician I desired to be, I needed to learn how to treat all three facets of a person's personality structure. God was broadening my quest for truth and reality. Studying God's design for personality theory is when I really began to get a deeper sense of awareness of the Bio-Psycho-Socio-Spiritual Dynamics of man. As humans, we are limited, but there is a reality that is unlimited; that is Omnipotent! That is why nothing works without God.

As doctors, we can medically treat the physical matter of the brain if there is a malfunction or disease attacking it. We can help the brain fire better. However, what we need to understand is that the mind is a function of the brain, it is <u>not</u> the brain. The mind of a person is where they experience emotions and make choices. We always have a choice and can learn to control our emotions, but there is not a pill that helps us learn to do so.

**We do not have to be impulsive
and we do not have to be angry.
We can choose to think more clearly,
and we can learn to make better choices.**

So within that context we can begin to understand what is going on within us. When I talk about the interaction of the body (Bio), the mind (Psycho), the social interactions of the environment (Socio), and the Spiritual because we have a relationship with God, I call it the "Bio-Psycho-Socio-Spiritual Dynamics" of human beings. It is plural because it is not static, it is always changing.

○ This "x" line of diameter represents one of the 360 degrees of unrighteousness, depravity, and worldly lostness of unregenerated man.

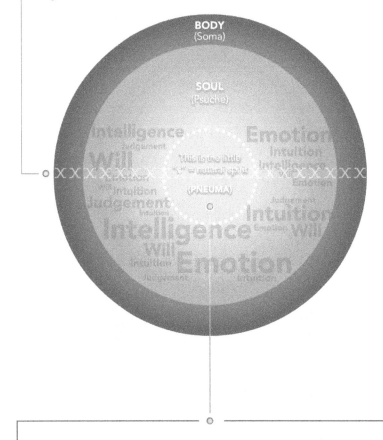

Dead to God in trespass, original sin. Has no righteousness and no means to generate the first smallest amount of righteousness in and of itself.

We have three circles in diagram D3 on page 9. The inner circle is the "natural or human spirit." In the Greek it is the *nephesh* which is the breath of God that gives existence.

The soul or the mind is the *psuche* in the Greek and from which we get our word psyche–psychology or mind or mental activity. I have mental activity or mind activity. As a human, in order to not only survive but thrive in life, I have got to try to make some sense out of that which often seems totally impossible. However, God is not a God of confusion. He is interested in me achieving an abundant and productive life. He wants me to know enough to be able to relate and understand more about Him, my relationship with Him, and His with me. He desires to give me the tools I need to not only function, but thrive during my life here on the earth.

The soul or mind houses our intelligence, judgment, will, and emotion. Intelligence has to do with the capacity to discern differences and comparisons. Intelligence is used in making judgments about the consequences of a particular choice of action. Judgment is the ability to discern or imagine the consequences and helps me weigh the risk between the facts that I know and the feelings that I am having. Our will then moves us into taking action. Our emotions are the influence exerted on all of these other areas and can come from the conscious or the unconscious realm of our minds.

Just the Tip of the Iceberg

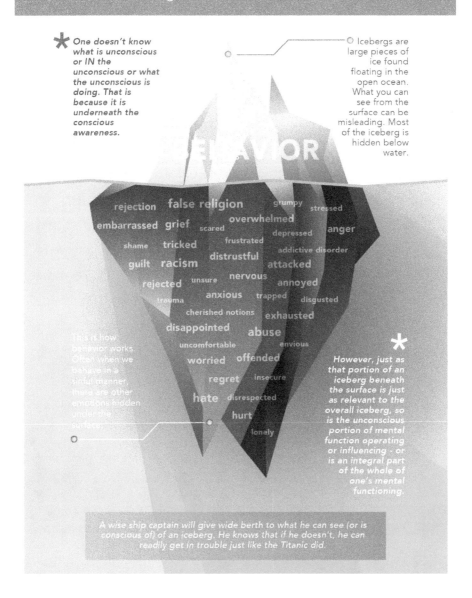

ICEBERG
Represents Conscious and Unconscious Aspects of
Mental Functioning Exhibited in Outward Behavior

One doesn't know what is unconscious or IN the unconscious or what the unconscious is doing. That is because it is underneath the conscious awareness.

Icebergs are large pieces of ice found floating in the open ocean. What you can see from the surface can be misleading. Most of the iceberg is hidden below water.

BEHAVIOR

rejection false religion grumpy stressed
embarrassed grief scared overwhelmed
depressed anger
shame tricked frustrated
addictive disorder
guilt racism distrustful attacked
rejected unsure nervous annoyed
trauma anxious trapped disgusted
cherished notions exhausted
disappointed abuse
uncomfortable envious
worried offended
regret insecure
hate disrespected
hurt
lonely

This is how behavior works. Often when we behave in a sinful manner, there are other emotions hidden under the surface.

However, just as that portion of an iceberg beneath the surface is just as relevant to the overall iceberg, so is the unconscious portion of mental function operating or influencing - or is an integral part of the whole of one's mental functioning.

A wise ship captain will give wide berth to what he can see (or is conscious of) of an iceberg. He knows that if he doesn't, he can readily get in trouble just like the Titanic did.

We can conceptualize our conscious and unconscious mental functioning by looking at the iceberg diagram on page 11. There is a portion above the surface that we are totally conscious of because we can experience it with our senses. We can see it, feel the temperature and the hardness, and we can even taste it.

However, there is another portion of an iceberg that is underneath the surface. We cannot see it, touch it, and are not consciously aware of it. However, just because it is outside of our awareness does not mean it is not just as much a part of that iceberg as the visible portion above the surface. As a matter of fact, there is often more underneath the surface than there is above the surface. Perhaps the portion under the surface is even of more significance because of how it is influencing the upper portion of the iceberg.

There are patterns of behavior in our minds that we may have pushed from the conscious level, for whatever reason, to the subconscious level or unconscious level. For example, somebody could know you well, see you two blocks away from the back, and say hello to you by name even though they cannot see your face. You ask them how they could possibly know it was you and they describe a specific way you walk. You are surprised by their description because you are not consciously aware of that particular mannerism. It is very obvious to others, but you are not aware you have developed that particular habit in your subconscious. It may be so far beneath the surface that you deny that what they are saying about you could be true.

There may be responses we have to circumstances based on past experiences that were real or perceived as real. There is a fear that was created by that event that we may have repressed so that we no longer realize why we respond or react the way that we do. A neurotic symptom is always a substitute for the actual root issue or problem whether we are consciously aware of it or not. If we have pushed it to the subconscious level, it is generally to make us feel better and less anxious. It is something we feel is too painful to deal with at the conscious level.

Failure to understand the three levels of our personality can cause us to be unable to handle life in a productive and abundant way.

Since only one-third of our personality is visible above the surface, we are in danger of destruction from the "iceberg" hidden beneath in the subconscious level. Only the light of God's truth can reveal not only the root of the problem, but provide us with the tools we need to deal with that root.

Truth and Reality

Truth and reality are one and the same thing. Fact is truth, if it is really real. It is not a notion about fact or my impression of it or a distortion caused by my unconscious. Even if I believe it, unless it is real, it is not a fact and it is not truth. Absolute truth is a fact that happens all the time, in all situations, with all people.

It is true for everybody. A myth is what happens for some people some of the time. In other words, it is relative; therefore, relativism is not truth. God says He is truth and that has to be the basis and core of it all.

Moehler says that the soul is between the spirit and the body. The spirit of man has the ability to hear the frequency of God or God's voice. However, there are other signals coming in distracting us so we cannot clearly hear God's voice until we are connected through Christ. We have to remember these influences are going on all around us all the time. Without Christ and the power of the Holy Spirit connecting us to God, we cannot be sure we are hearing correctly and staying on the right path.

If the captain of the Titanic had paid attention to the fact that you cannot just take what you see of an iceberg as total reality, he might have been able to safely navigate his ship. We cannot take what we are looking at consciously as the whole story! If we do not give credence to the possibility there is more to our mental activity than what we are consciously aware of, we are going to run into trouble.

The unconscious portion of our mental function is just as real as this conscious portion! Denying it is there is not truth and only leads to destruction.

God says He is truth, but the natural spirit is dead to God when the person is living in sin. There is no Holy Spirit and no Christ, so no connection with God. We say that we are fleshly, carnal, and in a state of sin. We are lost and cannot do anything about it in and of ourselves. Sin separates us from God.

So God says, "I will do it for you. You are separated from Me and you cannot grasp anything about Me because everything has to be spiritually discerned. I created you and I love you enough that I will provide what is necessary for you to have peace, comfort, and joy eternally."

Without God it is impossible to access what He has provided. Access is only available through Jesus Christ who said, "I am the way and the truth and the life. No one comes to the Father except through me" (John 14:6 NIV).

CHAPTER 1

Insights for You to Know and Apply

➢ *So if there is nothing worth dying for how can there be anything worth living for?*

➢ *Can I choose to think more clearly and learn to make better choices?*

➢ *Do I truly want the truth to expose the root of the problem?*

Action Steps

Without God it is impossible to access what He has provided. Access is only available through Jesus Christ Who said, "I am the way and the truth and the life. No one comes to the Father except through me" (John 14:6 NIV).

- *Will you surrender your life to God today and accept Jesus Christ as your Savior and Lord?*
- *Will you make God's truth the core foundation of your life by beginning to study His Word?*
- *Find a Bible-teaching church or class to help you discover the difference between truth and myth.*

CHAPTER 2

MAN — WHY A PSYCHIATRIC THEORETICAL CONSTRUCT FOR CHRISTIAN COUNSELING?

H ave you noticed that the unseen, immaterial part of life keeps forcing its way into our awareness? This reality fact is just one of the many dilemmas of the secular, scientific, biological approach to psychiatry, psychology, and other disciplines of counseling.

Many who study reality at the sub-atomic level state that apparently there is *"something more"* beyond even the eye of science. This *"something more"* is where Christian psychiatrists have an edge because they know what ultimate reality is and what an understanding of it can mean to the wellbeing of a patient. They have met the Creator personally through Jesus Christ and the Holy Spirit and have experienced that "beyond" reality which can powerfully impact the problems faced by their clients. Yet, for counseling at any level to have consistency and provide a commonly recognized mode of professional and academic communication, a common theoretical construct must be proposed from which any Christian counselor can work based on biblically accurate spiritual principles of truth and reality.

❧

When the answer is simple,
God is speaking.
-Einstein

❧

Rooted solely in a philosophical assumption of materialism, science offered up answers to the largest questions about reality. Science's theoretical construct of reality was proposed to be unassailable. Scientists thought they had a key to the creation of the universe and the source of life on this planet. This key was in particle theory based on electrons, neutrons, protons, and other sub-atomic particles.

The most recently discovered of which is the Higgs boson. It is the operant factor in the Higgs field which is believed to permeate all space and provide conceptually the "underlying matrix," if you will, of the universe. The boson is believed by some to be the last mathematically predictable particle in the Standard Model of Particle Physics. As all the other particles move through the Higgs field matrix, the Higgs boson's interaction with them is what gives them mass, or physicality. Because of this, and being consistent with their materialist worldview, it has been called by some the "God Particle." At the same time, many express their recognition and sense of need to explain *why* the boson is *required* to give particles mass and *how* this "interaction" of the underlying energy of each "particle" results in its becoming material, physical, weighable substance. Read more about this in chapter 4.

When the atom was broken down into its lesser components and those into their lesser components, the only thing ultimately left is what we identify as "energy." But what is energy? Is it material? If so, hand me a pound of it. Critical here is to understand the truth of "the actuality of the reality of immateriality." As demonstrated in the above comments, science itself affirms that energy, *per se,* actually (in reality/truth) cannot be weighed or measured!

To "explain" the atom, scientists continue to invent new names for new particles like "quarks," "w and z factors," "anti-quarks," "anti-matter," and "dark matter" to communicate about whatever their latest observations about the boson might be. However, describing an observation is not the same thing as explaining the source of, or the why of, its being.

Not that these factors are not evidential, it's just that as each is reduced, there is nothing but *energy* left. Thus each time scientists thought they were at the bedrock of reality in their materialistic conception – when they thought they had arrived at the final particle of particles — they found that there is yet *something more*: some other *something,* either even smaller or beyond man's capacity to even contrive to measure. In Reality/Truth, "Something" that/Who is immeasurable!

As the great scientist Galileo clarified several centuries ago, "Science can tell man much about how the heavens go, but can tell him nothing about how to go to heaven!"

We can't be sure, of course, what science will come up with next. Yet, it is amusing for those of us with a spiritual conception of ultimate truth/reality to imagine that if the scientific process continues to smaller and smaller bits of material, the end point of all this searching will be an assertion that so-called "physical" matter is nothing more than that which holds its "particles" together—energy.

Looking back, as a matter of science, we have been at this paradoxical point for decades. At the beginning of the 20th century, Einstein saw that mass and energy are equivalent and stated the equivalence precisely: $E=mc^2$. Thus, we can say that the materialistic worldview has been completely undermined by the pure science of which it is so proud. Pure science, the highest altar before which the materialistic/humanistic intellect for "knowing truth/reality" worships, has devolved itself to energy. The old metaphysical questions are loose again, even in and, especially, the world of physics. Many physicists are nonplussed by this fact, as was Einstein himself who believed in a God who "doesn't play dice with the cosmos."

Physics theory thus posits that energy bonds hold the *physical* "me" together. But these energy "bonds" which cannot be weighed and handed over as physical matter, *per se*, hold together the particles (which are no more than non-material energy bonds) of the atoms. When two or more atoms bond together, they form a particular configuration called molecules, which bond together to form a particular configuration called cells, and then tissues, which in turn are bonded or held together to form organs. These organs again are held together in a particular configuration called the body. It seems then that my body, like any and all things physical, is not physical at all, but is just a bunch, if you will, of "energy."

What About the "I" In My Body?

What, then, of even more subtle matters? Of what is the "I" or the "self" who inhabits my body *made?* And a not-irrelevant current religio-socio-political question: When and how did this "I" (which intuitively seems non-material) enter into this now "material" body? And, what is "my" ultimate destiny or purpose knowing this "material" body may not be *really/truly* what we have characteristically/traditionally understood as materially "real" after all? Or, what is the ultimate destiny of the "I" in my body that so intuitively seems to be even more non-material? These are the questions philosophy, religion, and psychology have been pondering since antiquity. Not only is this problematical, but it also provides a very practical way of approaching these "sticky" ideas.

Let me try to clarify with "reason" the concept of a "non-material body." In the usual way of thinking, I understand how such a concept presently can quite sensibly and accurately be seen as oxymoronic. Thinking colloquially and mundanely seems, however, to be how the *world* approaches thinking about most things including,

- "Where did I come from?
- What *is* life *per se?*"
- "What *about* death?"
- Also inherent in this question is, "What *is* death?"
- Another question of more pertinent relevance which is sensed immediately and piggybacks on the others with

an almost pleading demand to be answered right now is, "How might such considerations be of practical value to me here 'now' in the 'in between'?"

What's In It for Me?

In other words, if I recognize, acknowledge, and accept that there is "*something more*" than what pure science, humanism, and other materialist worldviews claim to be truth and reality, what's in it for me and what's it going to cost me?

When I asked the brilliant young training analyst if he was making the point that survival is the only thing that matters and he said essentially *yes*, I said to him and the audience, "Well if there is nothing worth dying for, how can there be anything worth living for?" Dead silence. This "*something more*" is what I was referring to.

It seems that this intuitive knowledge is common to all humans and is the source from which people throughout history had religion as a part of their cultures. They sensed within themselves that they needed *something more* beyond themselves to provide security if they were to "survive." History reveals the variety of the manifested forms of the expression of this—the erupting mountain, fierce beast, moon, or sun. These are something so far beyond humanity's own sense of *power to control* that it resulted in what we identify as a belief in *magic*. This was the stuff of idolatry in Biblical times and is still active today just in a more subtle form. This fact is the basis about which Freud wrote, "If there was no God, man would have to create one."

**A belief in magic is to believe that one can
perform something utterly impossible,
but is unconsciously believed to be personally
possible as *demonstrated* by *behavior;*
fulfilling the wisdom of the old adage
"actions speaks louder than words."**

We will hear more about how an active belief in magic is operative outside the person's conscious recognition as we discuss some of the case material such as obsessive compulsive disorder, perfectionism, narcissism, workaholism, drug abuse, anxiety disorder, dependent personality disorder [spousal abuse], depression, and more. A belief in magic, in fact, is what anyone who believes anything framed from any premise other than a materialistic orientation is accused of by the intellectual elite. [6]

This all derived in antiquity and actively persists today in the awareness of each person, at some level of their mental functioning, of a constant, unrelenting sense of vulnerability; that is to say, *an abiding sense* of *insecurity*. Insecurity implies the absence of the means to cause the body to survive, or cause it to continue

---

[6] It needs to be noted that a true and reasonable intellect will not shove aside as foolish the idea of *"something more."* Dr. Robert Jastrow, a self-proclaimed agnostic, was an astronomer, cosmologist, and a scientific leader at NASA for twenty years who died in 2008. He said, as a plenary speaker at a scientific meeting in Atlanta in 1994, "We, as scientists, should not claim that God does not exist. We can't prove that He doesn't, even as those who believe can't prove that He does." He was applying the intellectual integrity in the principle, "The absence of evidence is not evidence of absence."

to be alive, or stated more specifically, to not be dead! We will discuss the significance of what this means a little later.

As noted earlier, the Higgs field is thought or conceived to be the permeating matrix of all space, universal atmospheric space, our earthly environmental space, and the space between the organs, tissues, cells, atomic and subatomic particles holding together the "body." This phenomenon is the function of an expressed form of energy which can be understood as a type of mechanistic/"material" bonding.

In accordance with $E=mc^2$, we must remember all these particles, atoms, and molecules are just energy in particular configurations which we designate as mass or materiality. So, survival means the *soma* (the physical, material body) – all parts of which are just particular formations of energy — has not yet turned into other forms of energy, ultimately disappearing into what we call nothingness like a carcass does on the highway. Remember, energy can't be created or destroyed. Whenever the body "dies" – and whatever is the basis or bases for that phenomenon, and whatever it is or means (to soon be discussed) — it turns back into whatever it was before it came to be configured somehow or another into what is recognized as a physical, material body. If that's the whole story, and it's true that that's all there is, materialists have no problem.

What Is Life?

However, what about this thing we call *life*? And what about this thing we call *mind*? Each seems to be *in* or *associated* with the body, but neither is said to be a part *of* the body. In view of what I've presented so far, let's look at some definitions that speak to our subject matter:

Materialism: Noun: a way of thinking that gives too much importance to material possessions rather than to spiritual or intellectual things.

Philosophy: the belief that only material things exist. 1a: a theory that physical matter is the only or fundamental reality and that all being and processes and phenomena can be explained as manifestations or results of matter; 1b: a doctrine that the only or the highest values or objectives lie in *material well-being* [survival] and in the furtherance of *material progress* [humanism] (my emphases); 1c: a doctrine that economic or social change is materially caused—-compare historical materialism, 2c: a preoccupation with or stress upon material rather than intellectual or spiritual things.[7]

Naturalism defined, also, because it is an identical twin of materialism, just clothed in slightly different vestments:

1: action, inclination, or thought based only on natural desires, 2: a theory denying that an event or object has a supernatural significance; specifically: the doctrine that scientific laws are adequate to account for all phenomena.[8]

For the body of Christ, the Church, and its *Christ*-ian members, the Bible, throughout its entire content, not only challenges

---

[7] Merriam-Webster Dictionary

[8] Merriam-Webster Dictionary

this way of thinking, *but refutes* it as a habit pattern of thought, belief, and/or behavior. Pure science, humanism, and other materialists who believe, teach, and sincerely propagate this way of thinking are standing on much less firm, "proven" ground than they understand *even as they denigrate and disparage any other frame of reference* as they denigrate and disparage any other frame of reference as "unscientific" and, therefore, unintelligent, naïve, childish, and especially, *foolish*.

We are to be a "peculiar people," who talk and live differently because we think differently *from* and *about* the world JUST as Scripture states, "Do not conform any longer to the pattern of this world, but be **transformed** by the **renewing of your mind.**"[9]

Learning how to *think* differently as a habitual pattern must be practiced and developed, the same as any other good or bad, productive or unproductive, pattern so that it becomes habitual as a personal characteristic.

For our religion to *habitually influence* the choices we make, we must *practice remembering* the tenets and principles thereof. The Church doesn't seem to teach much about the reality of the spirit world. If the institutional Church were not so afraid to teach more about it Scripturally from the pulpit, perhaps, we

---

[9] Romans 12:2 NIV emphasis added

as Christian therapists/counselors wouldn't have as much business as we do. I am not talking about focusing on the devil and demonic activity, speaking in tongues or other languages, and the other gifts of the Spirit. Without nullifying or disparaging that part of God's Word in any way, let me state clearly that I am writing about the larger dimension of the reality of the *spiritual warfare* described in Ephesians 6:12 in which each individual is participating daily through his/her decision-making that is so influenced by his/her worldview, including especially that portion which is expressing itself *outside* of his/her awareness *unconsciously*! I will demonstrate this truth intellectually as well as clinically with the experiences of real people in real life toward the end of this book.

Spiritual Warfare

I'm trying, through the leading of the Holy Spirit, to illuminate the nature of the **spiritual warfare dynamics** operating in the personal battle each of us experiences in the exercise of our mental and emotional functioning within our personality structure arising from our own flesh as well as the other two enemy sources of temptation—the world and the devil. Without a deep awareness of these factors, we tend to lose sight of the battle and tend *naturally* to rely on our own strength.[10] Relying on human strength alone, we don't passively lose but, actually,

---

[10] "Thus saith the Lord; cursed be the man that trusteth in man, and maketh flesh his arm; and whose heart departeth from the lord. (Jeremiah 17:5)

actively choose to reject the availability of God's power and security to our lives.

As noted previously, philosophy, religion, psychology, and even science unknowingly and indirectly, have been pondering these questions since antiquity. However, to bring it to point, no rational intelligence would deny, for example, that there's a dramatic difference between a body in the coffin or grave and one that is engaged in writing or reading this page. Of what the nature of that difference consists is as huge a point of consideration as any looming before man's capacity to discern. The quandary permeating our very souls is, "Since my body is not 'me,' what then *is* the 'I' of '**me**'?" Unavoidably, a cohabiting question comes with it challenging, almost derisively, "And what difference does it make, if any, and what are **you** gonna do about it?"

Two of the most basic questions are clearly before us now. By the end of this book, I propose to have presented an intellectually satisfying and, therein, reasonable way of approaching each with an experientially functional resolution. Let's see now, however, if we can place a few more building blocks toward that purpose.

The Consequences of Relying on One's Own Strength

The more we personally rely upon our own strength, the further we miss the One Who gave Himself for us, that He might redeem us from all iniquity, and purify unto Himself a **peculiar** people, zealous of good works.[11] We tend to lose sight and forget

---

[11] Titus 2:14 KJV emphasis added

God's grace and our *dependence* on it as implied in the definition of who we are, "...a chosen race, a royal priesthood, a holy nation, a people for God's own possession, that *you may proclaim the excellencies of Him who has called you out of darkness into His marvelous light*; for you once were not a people, but now you are the people of God; you had not received mercy, but **now you have received mercy.**"[12]

We are not to be oriented only or even primarily to the world's mundaneness (Refer to diagram D4, page 30). Everyone should consider *how he or she arrives at the bases* for his own personal worldview.

**Each of us has a worldview from within which we operate whether or not we consciously think about it or believe we do!
This fact is inescapable.**

---

[12] 1 Peter 2:9-10 NAS emphasis added

God formed man from the dust. Made his material form - this is not what is made in God's image because God doesn't have a body. **Jn 4:24:** "I am Spirit;" and He has a soul. He thinks. He has a personality. He has feelings, attitudes, emotions, and He interacts. He has relationship.

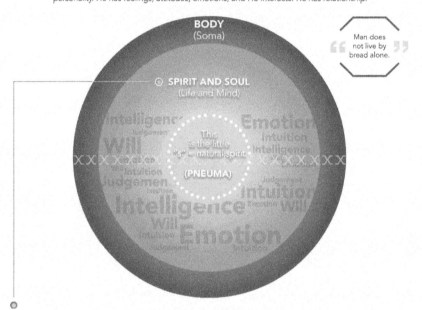

These two elements of man not put in yet, so he was not man or "human" yet. He had no life or mind "in" him yet. Not until God "breathed or Spirited into him" the Breath (Spirit) of Life did the material substance be made to be different from the atoms and molecules from the rest of the material --- now, it had a physiology, biology and biochemistry. It became "flesh" as soon as God added His image; i.e., His Spirit and Soul or Life and Mind to the material component which established personhood and potential for relationship. Inherent in His creation of man, God established that man have the power of his choices. Without that there could be no personal relationship. When God put some attributes of Himself into the created person man, He established man to be the only creature created in His image. That part of us that is in His image is our life and mind that He put into the material substance.

We must understand first that spirit and soul are not the same and can be identified separate, but can never be separated. As God says about Himself, "I am Spirit and I have a Soul." Secondly, we must understand that an image of something can never be the same as that thing. We must understand that spiritual reality is not actual reality or truth per se no matter how close. Pertinent to our cultural influences today, having been created in His image has many practical and theological implications. In fact, don't all theological issues have practical good goals? There was an ingredient or set of ingredients that were inherent in God (His image) that made Adam and Eve one with Him. Whatever that minimal set was that was essential for their oneness with God was lost at the Fall. However, there is a meme, memory trace or ingrain of that status or experience because there is an inherent universal awareness of a transcendency in all humans. It is manifested by man's tendency towards being civilized in spite of himself. And, more specifically by the universal fact that no culture ever recorded did not have a religion, an awareness of something or someone more than themselves to whom they turned near for security and hope for the future. It is this minimal element or set of oneness that is re-established at regeneration. It is and of God and He is the One Who re-establishes it. How that takes place is a point of inquiry.

Christians believe ultimate reality is the spirit world. God is Spirit (John 4:24). Spirit is non-physical. At whatever level we happen to be in contact with Him, God the Son, the Word in John 1:1-2, created what we call the physical world or the universe and all that is in it, by the power of God the Holy Spirit. So, the physical world and its operations (the laws of nature) is an *expression* of God, but is not God Himself. Having been "put" in a physical or material form, our body has no relevance to our having been "made" in GOD'S image. Genesis 2:7 reveals that God formed man from the dust of the earth. There was no life in that form at that moment. Not until He "breathed" or "spirited" into *that physical form* "the breath or spirit of life" did the body become *alive* (See again diagram D4, page 30).

It will serve us well at this point to learn a little more about the lexicology of the terms "breath" and/or "spirit." Two much published, highly reputable, contemporary neuroscientists, while discussing breathing in the practice of yoga, Andrew Newberg and Mark R. Waldman, in their 2009 well-received book, "How God Changes Your Brain," and under a sidebar heading of "What's So Spiritual about Breathing?" stated,

> "In western cultures, breathing would not be considered a spiritual activity but in eastern traditions it is the core of spiritual practice. Why? It's partially a matter of semantics. The Sanskrit word for breath is *prana*, but *prana* also means 'life force' or 'vital energy.' In the Hindu and Taoist traditions, the breath is also a metaphor for 'spirit' and

'soul.' Thus, by regulating your breath, you deepen your spirituality. Buddhism shifted the focus to the mind and devised breathing meditations that would give you greater control over mental and emotional states. This, it turns out, is neurologically effective. In eastern traditions, developing consciousness and mental control are genuine spiritual pursuits, and it all begins with the breath."[13]

The point about this is that the Hebrew words, *ruach* (spirit) and *nepesh* (soul), and the Greek words *pneuma* (spirit) and *psuche* (soul), to some extent connote the same lexical meaning of breath, life, and/or soul. In the next chapter on "God's Design for 'Theory of Personality,'" I will clarify and substantiate the practical meaning of these connotations relevant to the theme of our subject matter, i.e., "how we tick the way we do, and why we have so much trouble."

When the Elohim God Power, God's EGP, about which we will learn more in the next chapter, acted upon the inanimate subatomic, atomic, and molecular particles of the dirt, He transformed them into animate, living cells, tissues, organs, and operating organ systems which included, in place and functioning, all the biochemical and physiological systems into the body or *soma* and, it was good—meaningful, purposeful, worthwhile, and pleasing to God!

---

[13] Newberg, Andrew M.D. and Walkman, Mark Robert. *How God Changes Your Brain: Breakthrough Findings from a Leading Neuroscientist* New York: Ballentine Books, 2010

As clearly stated in the scriptures,[14] the consequence of sin was separation from God's qualitative characteristic of Eternality; so, an aspect of being created in God's image and of the oneness of Adam and Eve with God was lost at the fall. Mankind's source of security—God's presence, His loving *Yahweh, Elohim*, God power — was lost and humanity then became vulnerable to pain, suffering, and death. None of which he had ever been subject to prior to *choosing* to sin.

What Was the Most Basic Element of the Sin in the Garden?

At this juncture, let's take a look at the fall. God told them, "Don't eat of the tree of **knowledge** (of good and evil) in the garden, because if you do you will die!"[15] The serpent, the evil one, Satan, the devil, was there and he said to Eve, who looked upon the *fruit* of that tree and, from her limited, finite frame of reference—her limited capacity *to know*—saw it as appealing to look at, that it could satisfy appetite, and provide knowledge (the meaning of the word "science")–of good and evil. This is the very root of the tree, the knowledge of good and evil. And God, in His loving admonition, commanded, "You can have all you want of everything else in this garden, and *all you could possibly need is here*, **except** do not eat of *this* tree!"

---

[14] "But of the tree of the knowledge of good and evil, thou shalt not eat of it: for in the day that thou eatest thereof thou shalt surely die." (Genesis 2:17 KJV); "For the wages of sin is death..." (Romans 6:23 KJV).

[15] Ibid.

To clearly understand the pertinence of this event to our own lives today, we need to recall how Lucifer became Satan. I'll paraphrase Isaiah 14:12-15 here to make the point. Lucifer was the number one, head-honcho angel. He was the most beautiful, most intelligent, strongest, and most charismatic of all the angels. He was honored by God to be given this position of opportunity and responsibility. But he began to read his own "press clippings" and to say, "I will" rather than "Lord what is Your will for me?" He said four different times, "I will ...," then finally said on the fifth time, "In fact, I will become as the Almighty on high!" At that instant, he was thrown from heaven (Isaiah 14:12-15).

Why did God tolerate the first four "I will..." statements? Because, when Lucifer said, "In fact, I will become as the Almighty on high," he violated the first commandment God later gave Moses for us to adhere to in our relationship with Him, "Put no other god before Me!" Period!

Lucifer had become so impressed with himself, as he had come to envision himself to be — he felt he was the equivalent of God, the Creator of his very existence, and upon Whom his total wellbeing depended. He had just manifested what we as psychiatrists, psychologists, and therapists call "narcissism." As we examine of what it consists, we will discover that this narcissism is the very nature of sin itself. It is constructed of all that is involved in "I want to be as the Almighty on high! I want to be God!" I want no "excepts," no "no's," and no limits.

The Meaning and Relevance of the Concept of Narcissism

Freud coined the term "narcissism"[16] to refer to something he was observing in his patients as well as insistently operant in himself. He observed the inherent, indwelling of what he and others would come to designate as a drive. I have no particular objection to the term, *per se,* but I've come to simply characterize it as a habit pattern of reactional behavior, inherent across the board, in human beings. This **narcissism is simply the sin nature!**

All of us have seen this demonstrate itself in the earliest expression of being human. You can put two toddlers on the floor and give one forty-nine toys and the other one. The one with the forty-nine will not have played with half of those he has and wants the one the other has. And, he will not be satisfied without it! He wants it all. Wants no limits set. No exceptions. No "no's." In fact, I and every other one of us humans want, "What I want, right when I want it, just because I want it, and since it's *me* that wants it, I have a right to it!" The tendency to deny this truth about ourselves is one of the most destructive psycho-socio-spiritual habit patterns of reaction operating in our relationship with ourselves, with God, and as expressed in our behavior with one another. We'll see demonstrated examples of this later.

---

[16] Narcissism: *Microsoft Bookshelf Dictionary* (1996-97 edition)
    1) excessive love or admiration of oneself – conceit
    2) erotic pleasure derived from contemplation or admiration of one's own body or self, especially as a fixation on or a regression to an *infantile stage of development.*

Freud could not use the concept of sin nature because he did not believe in God or anything spiritual. Like other materialists, he believed that if you can't weigh or measure whatever, that whatever doesn't exist or isn't real.

Does Reality Really Exist?

Let's now explore the initial implications of the mindset that there is no actuality of the reality of immateriality, and initial considerations of the difference between goodness and righteousness. This mindset of "no actuality of the reality of immateriality" leaves us human persons with only man's valuation of everything to be true. This posits mankind, singularly, in the throes of ethicality and excludes him from *the hope that is in morality*, i.e. "*something more.*"

- Ethicality is man's valuation of what is real and true.
- Morality is an expression of God's valuation of what's real and, ultimately, the final knowledge of what is truth.
- Goodness is a corollary of ethics. Righteousness is a corollary of morality. Goodness is a corollary of materialism, i.e. man's valuing of his own capacity to do good, and not bad or evil.

From this ability, capacity, or power to judge, will, and effectuate, evolves in, or out of, the substance of his totally material self from which a belief system arises, he/she also then concludes that the brain is the mind. Righteousness is a corollary of spirituality, God's values, and virtues. Goodness and righteousness are not the same. The difference is the equivalent of that between light and darkness![17] I will discuss and clarify the critical significance this difference makes when we apply it to understanding the practicality of the "Psychology of Conversion" in my concluding thoughts.

Eve and Adam had never been subjected to temptation prior to each choosing to sin there in the garden. Eve accused the serpent, the instrument of Satan's purposes, of deceiving her. This was a second step of sin. It was an effort to deny the truth or reality of what had happened in the first instance. The fact was that she bet on her own intellectual prowess to know enough of the fullness of truth and reality to judge realistically what the adversary said, "Ah, c'mon now. Use your head. Use your intelligence. Does that make sense to you? Surely you won't die!"

This accusatory statement was in direct contrast against what God had said, "...don't eat of 'that' tree or you will surely die." In trying to hide behind having been deceived, she was trying to dilute and ultimately avoid responsibility of **her own choices**, by claiming deception. She herself was deceiving in an effort to deny the truth and reality of her own rejection of God as God. In that, she came from the same place Lucifer had. She put herself on the throne trying to usurp the "What and Who" of the character and nature of God's personhood.

---

[17] I am well aware of the philosophical discussions my comments might evoke. I am not, and do not claim to be, a philosopher. However, I stand by what I have presented. I do so unapologetically with relevance to the thematic purposes of this book.

Adam did the same thing by the ruse "the woman gave it to me," as if that removed the fact that he exercised his own intellectual judgment upon which he **chose** his volitional behavior, directly in contrast to what God had said to him personally.

Narcissism and Sin Nature

Our own worst enemy is "self." Eve and Adam were each relying on their own scope of intellectual capacity *to know*. Trusting in themselves to judge such issues, they also listened to and trusted the adversary's claim to know more than God. In that, they themselves claimed to at least be the equivalent of and/or know more than God. (If the pot can ever be or do what the potter can, the pot would actually be more than the potter!)

I want you, the reader, to more than weave together the psychological concept of narcissism and the spiritual concept of sin nature. The two need to become a coagulated understanding as one and the same phenomenon active in the expression of human character. When someone wants to hide his/her true identity, they use another name to deceive others.

That's the unconscious and unrecognized purpose of Freud's coining the name *narcissism*. From his limited scope of capacity to know, he did not want to refer or allude to anything that had to do with the spirit or non-physical world. He would have been acknowledging God if he had referred to sin, and then to heaven, hell, the devil, and all that crazy, unintelligent stuff! So, he coined the term narcissism to try to do away with the true identity of the most basic element of our being human, the sin nature.

In the "*something more*" of Christian psychiatry, the truth of its real name is identified in whatever guise it presents its self. Thereby, it can be recognized, can be acknowledged, and can be accepted to be the destructive ploy that it is. Reasoning declares the question, "If a person does not understand the nature of a problem, how can they possibly resolve the problem?" Moreover, when the truth is revealed, accepted, and not rejected, it **will** set the captive free.

I think it will be useful to further understand why Freud chose this particular term as apropos. Hopefully, it will contribute to understanding some of the bio-psycho-socio-spiritual dynamics operating in each of us and in the clinical material presented.

In Greek mythology, Narcissus was going to get a drink of water from a deep spring pool. As he leaned over to scoop the water, he saw the reflection of himself and said, "Man, look at that. I've never seen anything like *that* before!" And as he gazed at the image of himself, he became so enamored of his own image – again, *as he saw himself* — he went to embrace himself and drowned!

Does this sound familiar? It's the same dynamic Lucifer went through in becoming Satan, and, with the same results. It's the same dynamic taking place in the garden, just one or two more defensive maneuvers to try to deny or distort the truth, but it's all an attempt to serve the same purpose: to become as the Almighty on high. It resulted in destruction then, and it still does today. We will look at a few clinical examples later that are somewhat more complicated, but just as surely made up of the same attitudinal behavior and can be readily recognized as such.

The Breath of Life

So, God formed the materiality of man from the physical substance He had previously created by speaking it into being, by the Word of His "mouth!" (In quotations because God doesn't have a physical "mouth." We will treat the relevance of this later.) Having formed the "shape" from the smallest micro consideration of quantum physics and mechanics to the gross anatomical physiology, He imbued it with a quality of His own Spirit—"breath" (see Genesis 2:7). He would have us remember His loving admonition saying, "I am God, and there is no other; I am God, and there is none like Me!" (Isaiah 46:9).

He did not do this with any other of the physical, material substances He created without life in them, but this uniqueness of man included all of whatever else biological "life" has in it.

It is the presence of that "breath of Life," the quality of God's Spirit, that *"I am the Life"* quality that He *made* to be *immanent* with man as the provision to *exist eternally.* He also blessed us with the power of our own choice which is the *provision* for the *possibility* of having a *personal relationship* with Him. This relationship certainly seems to be what our existence is all about—to His Glory and our benefit! It was this quality that was lost at the fall, the very quality that provides *eternal security* in the oneness with Him. So the revelation, "For then [after death] the dust will return to the earth, and the spirit will return to God who gave it."[18]

---

[18] Ecclesiastes 12:7 NLT; Hebrews 12:9 NLT

Without this *essential quality* of spirit, only the physical — biological of "life" — quality remains that is also in all the other physical forms of life that are non-human. Man is left then to his own means (his "self" and his immediate environment) for security, all the faulty and inadequate forms of means which each of us personally are familiar, if we take an honest inventory. Since the fall then, man's cells, tissues, and organ systems operate on the same "biological" or "life" *principles* that the lower forms of "life" do and therein are, also, continuously vulnerable to frustration, pain, suffering, and ultimately to death! Thank God for the hope that is in Jesus Christ.

Thank God for the Hope in Christ Jesus

Ultimately, then, man's *eternal existence* will be either experienced in heaven in the presence of God or in the absence of oneness with God's presence, which is Hell. Interestingly, the materiality of all other physical creation is temporary, also, and is "groaning" and anticipating "that day" of the Lord's return.

> *We know that the whole creation has been groaning as in the pains of childbirth right up to the present time. Not only so, but we ourselves, who have the first-fruits of the Spirit, groan inwardly as we wait eagerly for our **adoption as sons, the redemption of our bodies.** (Romans 8:22-23 emphasis added)[19]*

---

[19] (cf. Philippians 3:21 NIV)

We need to clarify that there is a *real* and *irreducible distinction* between the *regenerated life* of those who belong to Jesus and the un-regenerated life of those who have rejected Him. Since the fall, all material substance, man's physical body, and the rest of physical creation, have been subject to destruction due to the pollution of sin in the world.[20]

Hebrews 1:6-7 says, "...Let all the angels of God worship Him...Who makes His angels spirits..." (NKJV). So the angels (like Lucifer and those who followed and fell with him) are created beings, also, but we are, again, different from them. They do not have bodies and, therein, do not have the option for salvation that we do in the <u>Incarnated</u> God, Jesus the Christ, Emmanuel (God with us), the Hebrew messiah–the Savior. Jesus <u>*performed*</u> His spiritual "Christ-ness" in and through the physical, material substance of His physical body relating to and involved fully in this physical world, but *without polluting His materiality with any sin*! "This High Priest of ours understands our weaknesses, for He faced all of the same temptations we do, yet He did not sin" (Hebrews 4:15 NLT). This is what "the hope that is in Jesus Christ" is all about. It is what makes regeneration, salvation, or being born again available as an *option of choice,* in faith, in the infallible gospel message of God's instruction book, the Bible.

---

[20] SECOND LAW OF THERMODYNAMICS: The life in plants and animals that was just "spoken into being" was not and is not the same as that that was imbued into human beings by God's "Breath or Spirit." God put some of His non-created Self into man that makes man eternally different than every other elective expression of His Creation Power.

What Is Spiritual Death?

Since the fall, the biological life in humans has been no different than that spoken into plants and animals — temporal only. This is in contrast to man's spirit and soul/mind that God put (breathed/spirited) into man as an element of His own *non-created* Self that maintains its unalterable and uninterrupted *eternality,* but has lost its assured eternal <u>security of oneness</u> with God for peace, comfort, and joy. This is the basis for the first death (being physical or biological death) and the second death (being spiritual death). As pointed out above, however, spiritual death cannot and does not mean cessation of existence since all *spirit* is eternal. Spiritual death is eternal separation from the Source and "Father of all spirits," God Himself. This separation from God is everlasting Hell.

Scripture assures us that there will be a bodily suffering component in Hell as well as that of the spirit and the soul, or "mind." As we'll see in the next chapter, just as all three components of the saved person's total personality—spirit, soul, and body—-are saved to participate in that salvation (1 Thessalonians 5:23 and 4:12; Romans 8:23), so will the *total* personality, all three components, participate in the experience in Hell — what it means to be unregenerate or *lost!*

We began this chapter with a question, "Why a theoretical construct for Christian psychiatry, psychology, and other disciplines of counseling?" Simply answered, because we have lost our security, and...

☙

We are powerless.

☙

Until we come to this awareness and recognize "the actuality of the reality of immateriality" we will continue to be insecure, powerless, and lost—unable to know who we are and _who we can become_. Therefore, we must turn our attention to understanding the only absolute Source of all Power – Who is "Elohim God Power (EGP)."

CHAPTER 2

Insights for You to Know and Apply

- _Learning how to think differently as a habitual pattern must be practiced and developed, the same as any other good or bad, productive or unproductive, pattern becomes habitual as a personal characteristic._
- _Each of us has a worldview from within which we operate whether or not we consciously think about it or believe we do! This fact is inescapable._
- _Sin elevates self to a position of having power and a claim that self is God._
- _We are powerless. All that is power resides in and belongs to God as EGP–Elohim God Power._

HOW DOES UNDERSTANDING THE *ELOHIM/YAHWEH* DYNAMIC ASSIST ME?

Of the basic traits common to being human, the bedrock and most primitive is a consciously or unconsciously perceived sense of insecurity.

As psychiatrists and counselors, one of our major tasks is to help our clients come to terms with the *reality* of the *truth* that there is *no security for life* in this world!

When a client's ability to adequately respond to his or her life's circumstances is sufficiently challenged, if **adaptive**, this root sense of insecurity stimulates efforts that may bring temporary relief. If **maladaptive**, however, a relentlessly increasing sense of vulnerability develops, expressed as clinical symptoms and/or syndromes. Helping clients effectively overcome such maladaptive behavior means getting at the root of that sense of insecurity. That root is exposed as they gain an increasingly adequate understanding of what I call the *Elohim/Yahweh* dynamic.

To discuss these concepts amply, however, we need first to differentiate between neurotic and organic symptoms. *Neurotic symptoms* are purely psychological and **always** involve *choice*. *Organic symptoms* are on a purely physical basis (anatomical, physiological, biochemical, or neuro-chemical) and, therefore, **have no option for choice.** With this understanding, let the following statement register indelibly as the *basic theoretical premise* of this Biblically constructed therapeutic method.

Every neurotic symptom is a direct expression or manifestation of the sin nature, in that it (the symptom) is a <u>maladaptive</u> effort (an effort, but one that never works or serves its desired, aimed at, purpose) to deny or distort the truth. It is maladaptive because it never works!

Whether the effort is to deal with a frightening, frustrating, or otherwise non-pleasurable experience (whether real or only *perceived to be*) the resulting symptom is a **maladaptive** effort; an effort, but one that never works because it does not reflect the reality — **or truth** — of life.

Like truth, reality refuses to be denied or distorted. It just will not and does not change. Denial or a distorted perspective results in missing the mark of Truth and Reality. Jesus asserted in John 8:32 that the Truth will set us free. The adversary *promises* freedom (or actually license) through something *always less than the truth*.

Aletheia–Truth and Reality

At this point, we need to remind ourselves that the Greek word *aletheia* means not only *truth in the abstract sense*, but also what is true in the sense of actual *physical reality*. God says *aletheia* — that which is Truth/Reality — will set you free. The reality of the Truth is that *there is no security* in anything or anyone in this physical world, especially and specifically **ourselves.** Each of us is vulnerable twenty-four hours a day to pain, suffering, and death. Pleasant or not, frightening or not, like it or not, each of us is **powerless** to find, gain, achieve, or provide security against the reality of this vulnerability! No matter how much the distortion or intensity of denial nor how we so defend and try to cling to "security," practical Reality repudiates the infantile wishful and magical belief that we possess our own "power."

What we try to substitute for *aletheia* by denial and/or distortion is supposed to demonstrate such "power" to *ourselves and others* and, thereby, relieve the angst that results from holding the Truth (of powerlessness) in unrighteousness (denial of Truth). What results is maladaptive behavior recognized by the therapist and others as the symptomatic expression of the underlying unresolved emotional conflict. Though these symptomatic expressions are certainly problematical, they are not the problem.

The problem is the underlying unresolved emotional conflict, the expressions of which are the manifest symptoms. If a person has tonsillitis, he runs a fever. This is certainly problematical and needs tending to for more comfort, and, in fact, one could possibly die from too high a fever. However, the fever is not the problem. It is just a symptom or manifestation of an underlying unresolved problem. If you focus on the symptom as if it were the basic problem, you never even recognize the nature of the actual cause of the problem and it goes untreated, thereby continues to have its effect even if the symptom is less impacting. If you never treat the infection, you never get rid of its influencing effects! The Apostle Paul gives us a Biblical analogy in Romans 1:18-20.

> For the wrath of God is revealed from heaven against all ungodliness and unrighteousness of men, who suppress the truth in unrighteousness, because that which is known about God is evident within them; for God made it evident to them. For since the creation of the world His invisible attributes, His eternal power and divine nature, have been clearly seen, being understood through what has been made, so that they are without excuse. (NAS, emphases mine)

The Wycliffe Bible Commentary expounds on Romans 1:18, "The righteousness and wrath of God both express divine action toward man. Righteousness is God's response toward faith or trust; wrath is His reaction to godlessness and unrighteousness. Both clearly reveal the response of God. What does a godless or unrighteous man do? He holds down or suppresses the truth (present participle) in the sphere of unrighteousness where he is living. He wants to avoid the truth about what he is, [powerless, vulnerable, AND NEEDY], and about what he is doing so he foolishly tries to get rid of, [denies or distorts], the truth." (Brackets mine)[21]

All neurotic symptoms are a direct expression of the sin nature.

That all neurotic symptoms are a direct expression of the sin nature was revealed to me about twenty-five years ago. A contemporary affirmation comes from Millard J. Erickson in his, "The Word Became Flesh, A Contemporary Incarnational Christology." In his chapter on "The Logic of the Incarnation," Erickson presents essentially the same notions about fallen human nature. He says,

> "We must remember that the empirical human nature with which we deal is distorted. It is possible that even some of the limitations of human nature which are not so obviously spiritual and moral were introduced or increased as the result of sin. For example, although human intelligence is presumably inherently limited, it may be that sin

---

[21] Gerhard Kittel, Editor; Translated by Geoffrey W. Bromiley. *Theological Dictionary of the New Testament;* (Grand Rapids, MI: Eerdmans) Vol. I, pp. 243-250.

limits our intelligence *and its functioning*, further hampering our understanding, *especially insight into spiritual matters*" (emphasis mine).[22]

Fear and hypersensitivity (i.e., tender emotional spots) not only stimulate unnecessary defensive attitudes and behaviors due to distortion and denial, but many times also erroneously nullify even the normal, healthy, God-given capacity to experience stress or anxiety evoked by awareness of actual vulnerability in real time and space. However, even in the face of emotional experiences, pragmatic Reality substantiates transcendence beyond ourselves. For Christians, that transcendence is the triune God.

Pragmatic Reality substantiates transcendence beyond ourselves. For Christians, that transcendence is the triune God.

Studies (Larson et al)[23] have shown that people of religious faith, whether "happy" Buddhists, Muslims, Shintoists, or whatever, have less stress, less illness, and heal better and quicker than those who have no religious faith. Of those of religious faith, however, Christians fare significantly better than all the others.

---

[22] *The Wycliffe Bible Commentary,* ElectronicDatabase (Chicago: Moody Press, 1962).

[23] *The Word Became Flesh. A Contemporary Incarnational Christology*; Millard J Erickson (Grand Rapids:Baker Books, 1991, p. 547.

No other religious group in the world has the historical Jesus, the Son in the triune Christian God. The Father *demonstrated His Transcendence* by resurrecting the Son's dead material body into an alive again — but altered — body that resulted in Jesus no longer having a material body but a spiritual body. Being supernaturally altered by Elohim God Power (EGP) and no longer being of subatomic, atomic, molecular, or physical, worldly substance, *His spiritual body was also no longer subject to the laws of nature.*

We should certainly not be surprised nor amazed at this because He clearly tells us in 1 Corinthians 15:50, "Now this I say brethren; flesh and blood cannot [i.e., under no circumstances] inherit the kingdom of God." The actuality of the reality of this fact about immateriality was demonstrated in several ways in His appearances to His disciples, but perhaps the most dramatic was the nullification of the natural law of gravity when He ascended (*floated up*) into the heavens, as testified to and recorded by many witnesses.

Without the peace-giving appreciation of who we are in Christ and of the all-powerful God controlling everything in the universe, we feel stress, dissatisfied, inadequate, defective, worthless, unlovable, unacceptable, have a marked lack of self-esteem and a sense of self-pity with anger, anxiety, depression, and feelings of overwhelming hopelessness. And rightly so!

Certainly, of course, not all we do to come to terms with Reality is maladaptive. However, all the various *defensive* maneuvers we do to deal with such feelings as mentioned above *are* maladaptive *for the very reason* that they are **defensive**. A defense is always against some perceived threat, actual *or not*. Since God promises "the truth *will* set you free," we are to learn that no matter how threatened we feel by the truth *of* any reality, or the reality *in* any truth, we do **not need to defend ourselves against** Truth *or* Reality. Rather, against all sense of threat or danger, we are to immerse ourselves in **attitudinal and behavioral surrender** to the **Transcendent One** Who is that **promise of security**! In other words, apply **faith** to our everyday living. Or, practice remembering to **do faith — what our religion is all about**!

Act Upon the Truth

As each of us knows, however, that's a lot easier to talk about than to do. Thank God for the hope that's in Christ Jesus, for He — in His humanity — practiced His (and our) religion by worshiping His (and our) Father, and His (and our) God.[24] He did just that for thirty-three plus years without one smallest failure before He died on the cross. So, throughout all His lifetime, He **performed** perfection, righteousness, and holiness. We need to comprehend that all three of these concepts, none of which we can do in and of ourselves, are lexically the same.[25]

In spite of all His human temptations, Jesus accomplished this in both the internal psycho-spiritual dynamics of His mental functioning (mind/soul) and the overt external activity of His

---

[24] John 20:17, Jesus said to her, "… but go to My brethren and say to them, 'I am ascending to My Father and your Father, and to My God and your God'" (NKJV).

[25] Leviticus 19:2, "Speak to the whole congregation of the Israelites and tell them, 'You must be (PERFORM) holy because I, the LORD your God, am holy'" (NET). Matthew 5:48, "So then, be perfect, as your heavenly Father is perfect" (The NET Bible).

body. Let whatever first comes to your mind serve as an example of a temptation He might have had to deal with and you will have hit upon one He did, in fact, deal with. He had to exercise faith against the tempting ideas in His mind and impulses He experienced in His body.

Because He knew man could not do it for himself and He knew the consequences of that failure, Elohim-Yahweh God, in His mercy said, "I'll do it for you through My Son. All you'll have to do is in faith proclaim Him before men and He will proclaim you before Me." As a substitute for us, He could not have closed that gap of imperfection or unrighteousness between us and God if He (Jesus) had not acted one hundred percent in faith in His relationship with the Father.

The operant relational factors that make this work are the same for each of us as those Jesus was referring to in John 17:19-23:

> *And for their [the apostles] sakes I sanctify myself,*
> *that they also might be sanctified through the truth.*
> *Neither pray I for these alone, but for them also*
> *[ourselves] which shall believe on me through their*
> *word; That they all may be one; as thou, Father,*
> *art in me, and I in thee, that they also may be one*
> *in us: that the world may believe that thou hast*
> *sent me. And the glory which thou gavest me I have*
> *given them; that they may be one, even as we are*
> *one: I in them, and thou in me, that they may be*
> *made perfect in one; and that the world may know*

that thou hast sent me, and hast loved them, as
thou hast loved me. (KJV)

There are varied questions frequently raised when speaking about **doing** faith and these beg for answers. How does one apply faith? A question often posed as "What are the righteous things one must do, feel, and think to apply faith?" The form of the question seems to reflect why there is as much difficulty in **being** more faithful; Lacking clarity about the underlying bio-psycho-spiritual dynamics we call our psychology, the form of the question seems to have the focus of emphasis reversed. The emphasis of these questions seems to imply that it is possible for righteousness to precede faith. To the contrary, any piece of righteousness done is an expression of faith in the **doing**. In other words, faith is expressed in or by a kind of action, as Jesus did, by performing some behavior internally or externally, either attitudinally or physically or both.

I understand the Scripture to say it is impossible to do, feel, or think one single righteous thing without first or, at the very least simultaneously applying faith.

Hebrews 11:6 states, "It's **impossible** to please God without faith" (emphasis added). In our relationship with God – on each and every occasion any one of us is in contact with Him — it is **always,** and **necessarily so**, over the bridge of faith!

Applying Our Faith

One of the main goals of this book is to try to help the reader learn more about how to apply faith (essentially, in spite of himself)! First by helping each person recognize how big a problem we humans have with doing even a single piece of righteousness. The magnitude of the problem seems not to be realized by the church in general, nor perhaps, therefore, by individual Christians personally.

Pragmatically, a priori, no one can actually do, accomplish, or fulfill the smallest piece of righteousness without **first** exercising **faith**. The righteous attitude or behavior must be effectuated experientially by the Holy Spirit — Elohim God Power — **informing and empowering the soul/mind** to a **cognitive understanding** in order for the individual <u>to even be able to</u> cognitively <u>choose</u> to carry it (the righteousness in attitude or behavior) out in the time/space of his/her functional life at any given moment or circumstance. The piece of righteousness is the result of exercising faith, not the reverse. We will explore this process much more in my concluding thoughts on the "Psychology of Conversion" and the clinical cases.

**It is impossible – it's not an option —
to please God without faith.
Righteousness is always coupled with
and dependent on faith.**

Whatever else positive or negative may be said about the thesis of this approach to understanding the application of God's Word to our lives, it certainly has been useful to many of the people I have had the opportunity to share it with over the years. This is the premise of why I say it makes perfectly good, common sense, that "God ain't stupid, and He ain't impractical."

As we move forward to that discussion, though, I need to establish a few more foundational stones which support the biblically spiritual principles that serve as the scaffolding for this theoretical construct for a Christian psychology and psychiatry. God's word can hardly be understood to be mere scaffolding, however. For the nature of His word is such that the least of it is the same as any other piece because of the complete wholeness in its total oneness of Truth and Reality. The next chapter speaks about the interactional and functional differences of the spirit, the soul, the mind, the heart, and the body. But, before we get there, some encouraging scriptural victuals:

1) "And he (Abraham) had **faith** in the Lord, and it was put to his account **as righteousness**" (Genesis 15:6 Bible in Basic English emphasis added).[26]

2) "By faith, Noah became heir of the **righteousness** which is **by faith**." (Hebrews 11:7 KJV emphasis added).

3) "...for we say that **faith** was reckoned to Abraham **for righteousness**" (Romans 4:9b KJV emphasis added)

4) "...well, we have been saying that Abraham was counted as **righteousness** by God **because of** his **faith**" (Romans 4:9 NLT emphasis added).

---

[26] https://www.gotquestions.org/Bible-Basic-English-BBE.html

The focus of this book has been, is, and will be to help discover the "how to" (bio-psycho-spiritual dynamics) and the measure (results) of receiving the power-love of Elohim-Yahweh God into your life through faith and what (considering particularly) interferes with it.

The French Philosopher and mystic, Simone Weil, envisioned it this way. "It is only the impossible that is possible for God. He has given over the possible to the **mechanics of matter** and **the autonomy of his creatures**" [my emphasis].[27] She also stated, "I am not a Catholic (i.e., Christian); but I consider the Christian idea, which has its roots in Greek thought and in the course of the centuries has nourished all of our European civilization, as something that one cannot renounce without becoming degraded."[28]

Additionally, she also recognized the tenet of Biblically Christian psychology that I am here espousing. To surrender to the fullness of Biblical Truth and Reality is to gain peace, comfort, and joy even in malignant circumstances. She stated, "In struggling against anguish one never produces serenity; the

---

[27] Simone Weil (1909-43) "A War of Religions" written 1943; published in *Selected Essays*, ed. by Richard Rees, 1962.

[28] Letter, March 1937 published in Simone Petrement, Vie de Simone Weil, vol. 2, ch. 3, 1976. The Columbia Dictionary of Quotations is licensed from Columbia University Press. Copyright © 1993 by Columbia University Press. All rights reserved. Caedmon recordings reproduced by arrangement with Harper Collins Publishers.

struggle against anguish only produces new forms of anguish."[29] The surrender is not to some impersonally conceptualized "force," however. It is in the context of an interactive and **personally experienced relationship** with the One Who not only **has ALL power, but IS All THAT IS POWER** (Psalm 62:11)!

Defensive behaviors to attain personal security against physical injury or death are no longer urgently, frantically sensed to be necessary when there is such confident surrender to proclaimed verbal truth that has also been **demonstrated** in physical reality as **testified to by so many witnesses** (Luke 1:2; John 1:14; Acts 1:3 and 4:10; 2 Peter 1:16-18; 1 John 4:14). Indeed, for Christians, peace, comfort, and joy are to be found **even in the face of life-threatening vulnerability.**

God's Power Brings Peace

One of my own "peace that passeth all understanding" experiences with God happened in 1980. My wife and our two youngest sons were on our way fishing for the weekend. I was driving on a long slow curve and noticed a vehicle afar off coming at me a little bit on my side of the road. My wife happened to ask me something about that time and I turned to speak to her. When I turned back, this vehicle was wholly on my side of the road. I moved over to the roadside at which point he followed. I said to myself, *"Well I'm not going to just let you run right into me."* I veered suddenly back to the highway and he tragically did the

---

[29] Draft of letter to Andre Weil 1940; published in Seventy Letters, pt. 2, no. 39, 1965.

same thing at the same time and we had a head-on collision in my lane. I was unconscious just a fraction of a moment and then fully conscious, alert, and aware of everything going on. What I'm going to relate was all going on at the same time and seemed longer than it probably was.

I immediately found myself talking to God. I said, "Lord I really don't understand this and why it's happening. Everything was so good, not stressful, and happy, but it's okay." Then I saw my wife lying unconscious with her head on the seat with the left side of her face looking like a bloody pulp and gurgling as she breathed. I said, "Lord, You know how it will affect my life if she dies, but it's okay."

As that was taking place, I was also trying to determine why I couldn't see out of my left eye. Something was hanging down in my face. I first thought it was a part of my frontal lobe hanging there. A person could have a frontal lobe injury and still be conscious. I felt my skull and it was intact so that was ruled out. I then thought it must be my eyeball hanging there, so I moved it and I could then see. The fact was that a slab of nose, eyebrow, and forehead skin was torn and hanging there.

I'd been able to observe the boys to be essentially okay. The older one had a laceration on his forehead and a concussion, and the younger one who had been lying down in the club cab back seat had a severe concussion. When I was braking and dodging, he raised up and on impact the boat flew forward off the trailer and hit him in the head when it caved in the back of the truck cab.

The circumstances were worse for me, however. Gasoline was pouring everywhere. I was trying to get to where I could help my wife, but I was jammed down between the steering column and the left sidewall under the dashboard. I was stuck, realized I was hurt pretty badly, and the more I struggled the worse it became, but I had to get to my wife. When I put my hand down where I was hung up I thought my left femur was fractured and the bone had come out and stuck into the seat. I was finally able to move a particular way and became dislodged. What I thought was my femur stuck in the seat was actually the emergency brake which had impaled my left buttock. My left hip was fractured along with several other bones.

As I was impaled and trapped there with the gasoline fumes engulfing everything, I said, "Lord, You know dying by fire has always been my most dreaded way to die. I don't really understand all this, but it's okay."

This was a very, very bad tragedy. The driver of the other vehicle was a nineteen-year old young man who died there also trapped in his truck. He died loudly cursing God. He had two mid-teen little girls with him, each seriously injured for life. They later acknowledged he had previously run two other cars off the road. There was purported to be alcohol, marijuana, and other drugs involved, as the two girls required no further sedation while being diagnosed. My wife, sons and I went through the long-term process of recovering from our serious injuries but not without some residual physical, mental, emotional and financial impact from the entire experience.

This "any day experience" in my life examples how our relationship with God, in Christ, is **ever present** and can be so useful in dealing with not un-commonplace occurrences that can take place at any time in any person's life. I want to say again, though, that God ain't stupid and He ain't impractical, faith doesn't seem to be to knowingly invite danger or enter into a dangerous situation without a realistic evaluation of valued consequences or "outcome-to-risk" of physical, mental, and spiritual welfare.

Responding in Faith and Receiving His Peace

In other words, there is a difference between tempting the Lord and acting or responding in faith. Handling (and mishandling) poisonous snakes is an effort to tempt the Lord into proving His presence, power, and faithfulness. It is an unrecognized effort by the doer to "demonstrate" to himself and others that he is in control of his life's circumstances and, in fact, his very life — and dies. This is a maladaptive effort to distort and deny the Truth. This sort of thing never works because the Truth of God will not be distorted, denied, or manipulated. To run across the freeway saying, "The Lord will protect me," is not an expression of faith. It is a maladaptive effort to distort and/or deny the Truth and, at the very least, awfully unrealistic.

With common sense, I am not proposing any unrealistic, magical notions about not trying to lessen or remove any real threat or danger to one's person. In the wreck, I was trying my best to get myself and my family out of the danger we were in. Had the gasoline ignited, I would have tried even harder to extricate myself.

Had that happened, and I knew full well it could, we all would have died tragically and without apparent reason. However, "the peace that passeth all understanding" was afforded me by God's grace to a believing faith in His promise: "For I know the thoughts that I think toward you, says the Lord, thoughts of peace and not of evil, to give you a future and a hope."[30] I believe Jesus accomplished that through His performing of one hundred percent faith for me and anyone who will in gratitude and faith receive it.

One of the things we can absolutely bank on in this life is that everything "ain't always gonna be okay, but everything is gonna be okay," especially for a Christian — **even unto death!**

The truth is that security lies only in the EGP of God in Christ.

---

[30] Jer. 29:11 NKJV

D5 | Describes the Practical Application of the
BIOPSYCHOSPIRITUAL DYNAMICS

⊙ Where the operation of the mental functions of:

Intelligence, Judgement, Will, Emotion, Intuition

take place

BODY
(Soma) Greek

⊙ **SOUL**
(Psüche)

NATURAL

little "s" = "spirit" dead to God in trespass. Needs to be regenerated or "born again" [when] man's spirit - the Holy Spirit then being present informs man's soul (See note)

NOTE: the power and love - EGP (Elohim God Power) and agape love which only the Holy Spirit can provide and the capital "S" vs. the little "s" designates metaphorically. Here is a time to look at the Psychology of Conversion. What takes place to convert, change, transform the little "s," which has been there from the instance of the Fall to the first moment in time that God instituted and effectuated His plan of redemption, resulting in the little "s" being transformed into the capital "S."

Upon regeneration, we are no longer bound **to** sin, because we are no longer bound **BY** our sin nature. We have been freed from sin, but we are still free to sin. Such a sense of security is the result of the effectuation of *Elohim God Power ("EGP")* (See diagram D5 on page 63). This is the dynamic of the relationship with God **in** Christ. Before regeneration, I was unable to choose **not** to sin. I had no option because of the depravity of my own sin nature. I also had no way of doing even one piece of righteousness in and of myself (Isaiah 64:6). Thank God for the hope that is **in** Christ Jesus.

When *Elohim God Power*, this EGP, is appropriated and becomes real in us, it results in our being born again and reconciled to the Creator God by the Holy Spirit Himself "washing" and regenerating our spirit, restoring the oneness with Him lost at the Fall. At the same time, having Christ's Advocate, the Holy Spirit, *in* our spirit also effectuates a **renewing** of our mind; that is to say, how we think influences how we feel — the spirit is the vitalizing, fueling element of the soul (or mind).

Our previously lost — or dead to God — spirit, in its singular carnality, left the soul (or mind) to its own **limited** and, therefore, impotent and ineffectual devices toward gaining security. Being regenerated — or born again — by the presence of Christ's Holy Spirit, the Christian's spirit now has an element available to itself able to fuel the soul's (mind's) executive choice-making function with empowerment to be "spiritually minded." To be carnally minded is death, but to be spiritually minded is life (Romans 8:6).

Insights for You to Know and Apply

- *Every neurotic symptom is a direct expression or manifestation of the sin nature, in that it is a maladaptive effort to deny or distort the truth.*
- *Pragmatic reality substantiates transcendence beyond ourselves.*
- *For Christians, that transcendence is the triune God.*
- *Without the peace-giving appreciation of who we are in Christ – the "ALL POWER" God controlling everything in the universe — we feel stress, dissatisfied, inadequate, defective, worthless, unlovable, unacceptable, have a marked lack of self-esteem, and a sense of self-pity with anger, anxiety, depression, and feelings of overwhelming hopelessness.*
- *Real and lasting security lies only in the EGP Power of God in Christ.*

IS THERE INDIVIDUAL RESPONSIBILITY?

In this chapter we will address common terms like body, soul, and spirit. These terms are frequently referred to in the Bible, also. Of the group, "body" (materiality) is probably the most understood with any general conceptual sense of appropriate accuracy. When asked, "What is the body?," one can answer objectively by presenting his own body, a photo, or a mirror, and each to which the senses can be applied for the formulation of a concept of "body" – all having to do with physical, materiality. As alluded to earlier, the materialist also would equate "heart" as referable only to the physical organ. In addition, the materialist necessarily claims that the physical organ, the brain, is the mind. (As we progress, I will show it is not.)

However, for the most part, the understandings for usage of the terms spirit, soul, mind, life, and heart are rather non-definitive and have an almost ethereality with a rather loose reliance on the intent of its usage to be gained from its context. There seems to be an attitude that "everyone understands what that means," and the conversation moves on with a more or less tacit agreement to let it go at that. Quite honestly, however, important clarification of terms can easily clear up or prevent misunderstanding.

Neither the Hebrew of the Old Testament nor the Greek of the New Testament make the task for clarity much easier. As I study the scholars, there are differences of opinion amongst them, from the fathers to the present day, and sometimes rather strongly. There are *several different words* in Hebrew and Greek for these terms that lexically are translated legitimately into the English language, but each has the burden of conveying the same connotations and meanings as its counterpart in the other language. This problematic burden leads to our present discussion.

I want to emphasize I am not trying to enter such a lexical debate within the purpose of this book. However, I do have the responsibility to clarify the primary terms used in our considerations of the book's subject matter for the purpose of its understandings to be applied worshipfully "in spirit and in truth." The more we can *real*-ize that God's Word is the most practical book ever written, and it's the best "how to" book going, and it's the **instruction book** about how to get along in this stinking world with our stinking selves, the better off we'll be. We will have learned more about how to be our own best friend rather than our own worst enemy. To operate to the contrary is not intelligent or smart, and, in fact, is dumb, so, "...let he who has ears... hear..." (Mt. 11:15, 13:9, 13:43; Mk 4:9; Lk 8:8, 14:35 NKJV)

Less understood of the group of terms are "spirit" – or the soul; "life" – or the mind; or "heart." The physical senses cannot be utilized at all to the same clarity as they are for the gross comprehension of "body" because it, and all its various organs, is material substance. None of the others are of a physical nature yet are as comprehensively actual as the material body is real or actual.

Of all the terms we want to clarify, the word "heart" perhaps is the most loosely translated. As a parable's meaning is understood indirectly, so it seems it is with the word "heart." The author Andrew Malone quoted the eminent 17th Century Old Testament scholar, John Owens, saying, "In the words of Owens, the heart in Scripture is variously used, sometimes for the mind and understanding, sometimes for the will, sometimes for the affections, sometimes for the conscience, sometimes for the whole soul. Generally, it *denotes the whole soul of man and all the faculties of it,* not absolutely, but as they (all the faculties) are all *one principle of moral operations,* **as they all concur in our doing of good or evil."** (My emphases)

I concur that all the faculties are of one principle of moral operations, but it is not accurate that they all concur in our doing good or evil. If they all concurred in agreement, Paul would have had no basis upon which to write Romans 7 because there would be no conflict, no spiritual *warfare,* no neurotic behavior, and no reason to write this book. All and every faculty in whatever makes up man's personality structure is involved in the choices he makes. By the grace of God there are non-concurring elements in the "faculties" in the "soul" that make up the whole of God's chosen structure for man's total personality–spirit and soul and body.

Quite concretely the word heart refers to the physical organ. Colloquially we use it metaphorically saying, "It was from his heart" or "He gave his heart to her," to convey the measure of a person's *sincerity at the deepest level of their inner being, their "bowels," their "gut," their "heart," their "soul."* In the Bible, it's most infrequent usage refers to the organ; it's most frequent usage seems to be the result of the collocation of the words spirit and soul. Each is a distinguishing term, but, linguistically, if you juxtaposition them closely, side-by-side, their meanings become relatively indistinguishable. Again and to further punctuate, my years of study and experience have convinced me that the Bible is the most practical book ever written, the best "How To" book going, and the best "Instruction Book" about how to get along in this stinking world with our stinking selves. With God's grace and the leading of the Holy Spirit I am trying to be helpful to the reader **toward** a deeper understanding of the instructions so we can better carry them out to God's glory, but also to our own so-needed benefit.

> *"Then the* LORD *saw that the wickedness* (the attitude and behavior resulting from the choices exercised in the economic flow of the bio-psycho-spiritual dynamics that take place in the interaction of the components of the total personality structure of man – spirit and soul and body – and each contributing) *of man was great in the earth, and that every intent* (purposed planning) *of the thoughts* (attitudes, intents, and behavior arrived at – wickedness) *of his heart* (that is, at his deepest level of sincerity) *was only evil continually. And the* LORD *was sorry* (mental or emotional attitude) *that He had made man on the earth, and He*

*was grieved (*mental or emotional attitude) *in His heart (*collocated soul and spirit)." (Genesis 6:5-7 NKJV) (emphasis added).

It may be helpful if we can conceptualize the "heart" as a funnel into which all the "faculties" of each of the structural components — the spirit/life, soul/mind, and body — contribute. However, there are also other influencing factors impinging on each of these. We live in a social, political, economic, religious, and physical environment, each one of which that challenges each component of each individual's personality. The positions, beliefs, and goals of others — which we can designate as "wants" of every "other" (thing or person) — are not going to be the same as mine. The psycho-spiritual activity we call adjustment, accommodation, and adaptation each is a method of attempting to deal with the challenge of the difference between two "I's" — mine and another's.

The problem inherent in each "I" and to which each "I" contributes is and arises from when each "I" wants what he or she wants and what he or she wants is different. We each want what we want right when we want it and both feel we have a right to it! We are offended if it is not immediately *forthcoming.*

This brings us to be able to consider the most pertinent and prevailingly pervasive understanding we need to heed about the "heart" – stated not inexactly and without any equivocation in the following verses:

The heart is deceitful above all things, and it is exceedingly perverse <u>and</u> corrupt and severely, mortally sick! Who can know it [perceive, understand, be acquainted with his own heart and mind]*? I the Lord search the mind, I try the heart, even to give to every man according to his ways, according to the fruit of his doings.* (Jeremiah 17:9-10 AMP) (emphasis added).

And He said, "What comes out of a man, that defiles a man. For from within, out of the heart of men, proceed evil thoughts, adulteries, fornications, murders, thefts, covetousness, wickedness, deceit, lewdness, an evil eye, blasphemy, pride, foolishness. All these evil things come from within and defile a man." (Mark 7:20-23 NKJV)

But you have not so learned Christ, if indeed you have heard Him and have been taught by Him, as the truth is in Jesus: that you put off, concerning your former conduct, the old man which grows corrupt according to the deceitful lusts, and be renewed in the spirit of your mind, and that you put on the new man which was created according to God, in true righteousness and holiness. (Ephesians 4:20-24 NKJV)

This is some of the stuff from which spiritual warfare is spawned. In and of our natural selves we have no chance of overcoming it. Thank God for the hope that's in Jesus Christ. I will next discuss Elohim God Power – EGP and its relevance to our problems and their resolution.

What of Who God Is? Is God Supernatural, Natural, or Both?

Moreover, inherent to the task of this book, it is necessarily helpful to conceptualize the correlation of the terms supernatural and natural by thinking about "What of Who" God is in relation *to* us, and vice versa. Doing so, then, ponder the gracious fact He affords us His having a relationship *with* us and allows us to be involved in that relationship in such a way that we, in truth and reality, have a personal relationship *with* Him. The mundane, practical usefulness of such considerations is *to help ourselves think about* the why and the "how to" of removing the barriers against the oneness of God's immanence *in* us and His transcendence *to* us! Each time we *do* a piece of *faith*, that removal of a barrier against the oneness with God's immanence and His transcendence has just been accomplished.

By His grace of forgiveness and coming into a person's (soul's) life (spirit) and thereby regenerating (beginning again – anew) that spirit or life, the soul's (mind) activity of decision-making is now empowered to surrender that person's spirit, soul, and body to trusting the What and Who of God – in that, there is closure to the oneness of natural with the supernatural. Through this the supernatural is pragmatically demonstrated to be the only real truth because such closure to oneness can't be done from the other direction – from the natural to the supernatural. Science and other materialistic ideologies are impotent to effectuate anything like that because they are not Truth or Ultimate Reality! They are as those who "have a form of godliness, but deny the power (EGP–Elohim God Power) thereof" (2 Timothy 3:5 KJV).

God Is Love and Defines Love; Man Does Not! God Is Power and Defines Power; Man Does Not!

The Bible teaches that the spirit and soul and body are real and speaks clearly about the relationship of each to the other. However, the most incisively poignant piece of practical intelligence to be derived from its teachings is that the one – the spirit realm — **cannot** be reached or even approached from the other — the material or physical realm. The material came from and is utterly dependent on God, Who is of the immaterial realm. Nothing about God is physical or material. He created all that is material or is of Nature or "natural." Therein, He is not limited by the laws of nature. He created them! (We will speak more about this when addressing Elohim God Power – "EGP".) He can violate or overrule any and all of the laws of nature at any moment in time or space that He chooses to. That's what miracles were and are. In John 10:38 Jesus said, "But I do them, even though you do not believe Me or have faith in Me, [at least] believe the works and have faith in what I do [what you see Me do], **in order that you may know and understand** [clearly] that the Father is in Me, and I am in the Father [One with Him]" (AMP emphasis added).

Does God have a body? God has just clarified that the qualitative characteristics that designate humans to be the only creatures created in His image cannot possibly have anything to do with our bodies.

God doesn't have a body! He is Spirit! However, He thinks, feels, and speaks of His soul, also; so He has Personhood (another quality of Himself), some of which He imbued in us when He created us in His image. He created the material, formed some of it in the shape of the body, breathed (Spirited) into it and man became a living soul (or *person* as the NIV and others state it) that, due to the inseparability of the two — spirit and soul — was *inherently* and, therefore, simultaneously imbued with *life* to vitalize, invigorate, energize, and empower the activity or function of mind (soul), which we identify altogether as personality.

Let's look closely at Jeremiah 29:11 to try and grasp what God wants us to gather into an experiential understanding. But, because it also relates, let's first carefully consider Jesus' promising proclamation in John 10:10, "I have come that you can have life and that more abundantly." God gives us a great deal of information to help us experientially recognize and better comprehend some aspects of Himself — His Personhood and His personality that most people seem aware of, but more or less take for granted. Jeremiah's verse punctuates not only the significance of the practical value of these aspects of God but affirms, possibly indirectly, that that part of *our* personality structure made in His image is spirit and soul.

These two verses are as proclamation promises. "I am continually consciously aware of the plans I have toward, about, and for you. For all who 'have ears to hear and eyes to see' and have received My Son, through Whom we are one,[31] I can and do promise to give or provide 'life abundantly,' not only because I "have" it to provide or give, but because the verity of this Truth is because REALLY, 'I AM' IT!"

Let's look at four different Bible presentations of Jeremiah 29:11 as it relates to John 10:10:

> "For I **know** the *thoughts* that *I think* **toward** *you*," says the LORD, "thoughts of peace and not of evil, to **give** you a *future* and a *hope*" (NKJV).

> "For I know what plans I have in [My] **mind** for you," says Adonai, "plans for well- being, not for bad things; so that you can have hope [**for now**] and **a future (the hereafter)**" (CJV emphasis added).

> "For I know the thoughts **and** plans that I have for you, says the Lord, thoughts *and* plans for welfare **and** peace and not for evil, to give you **hope [now] in your final outcome (the "ultimate reality" of the spirit world)**" (AMP emphasis added).

---

[31] "I am the way, and the truth, and the life. No one comes to the Father except through me" (John 14:6).

"For I am conscious of my thoughts about you, says
the Lord, thoughts of peace and not of evil, to give
you hope at **the end**" (BBE emphasis added).

First He identifies Himself in His separate individuality with
the words "I" and "My." He also declares, affirms, and acknowl-
edges the separate individuality of each one of us with the word
"you." He stated in John 4:24, He is Spirit and, therefore, has no
body, which implies having no brain. He indisputably affirmed,
however, in Jeremiah 29:11 that He thinks (has a mind), has
(IS) knowledge, is conscious of, and remembers purposeful plans
He has devised for us. In this He ratifies that He and we have a
relationship!

Wishful, Magical Thinking Seemingly Satisfying Powerfulness

In our created "being," we "are!" Like it or not we cannot "not
be." Killing one's body does not end the "being" of one's "personhood." The spirit and soul can be individually differentiated but
are inseparable. Being in His image, the **consciously mindfulness of the spirit** is the operant expression of that inseparable
relationship between the spirit and soul (further discussion of
this concept a little later). The very notion of having the option to
stop "being" is only a wishful fantasy to be in control (or to have
power) which, according to God and literal experience, is not
an option at all. Remember Psalm 62:11 which says, "All power
belongs to God." **All** of whatever **power** is belongs to God (EGP:
We will deepen and broaden our understanding of this Scripture

and its critical import for biopsychospiritual balance and health in life as we move further along)!

Materiality Is Limited; Immateriality Isn't!

As our incapacity to stop "being" is directly related to God's characteristic of being All Power, so also is another qualitative characteristic of His nature relevant to the same reality truth—God's eternality. Our spirit/life and soul/mind, each being like His, excludes any materiality—-in any of which we must note inherently entails temporal limitation. **The actuality of the reality of the immaterial spirit/soul world has no such limitation.** Though incomprehensively inconceivable to us, the immaterial world is timeless and formless. It is and was everlasting, and infinitely **eternal.**[32] Yet demonstratively real! This must become your worldview.

Jesus lovingly admonishes us in Matthew 10:28, "And stop fearing those who kill the body but do not have the power [EGP] to kill the soul." His words, of course, were not just for the understanding of those who heard Him then, but perhaps the socio/cultural senses of our day are even more needful than they were. However, He concludes for them and us, saying, "But rather be fearing Him who has power [EGP] to bring both soul and body

---

[32] John 1:1-4 says, "In the beginning [before the world was] was the Word, and the Word was with God, and the Word was God. He was [before the universe was] in the beginning with God. All things were made through Him, and without Him nothing was made that was [or has been] made. In Him was life, and the life was the light of men." (Emphases added.)

to the condition of utter ruin[33] and everlasting misery in hell."
(Wuest NT emphasis added)[34]

In John 1:1-14[35] and also in Matthew 1:23 that Jesus is the
God-man Savior Christ; Emmanuel, which name means "God
with us!" **Before** the "beginning" God —- the "I Am" of Exodus
3:14 and John 8:56-58 —- was! God's image in us is our spirit
and soul imbued with the qualitative feature of eternality as an
element from the Elohim creation power of God Who makes our

---

[33] I specifically chose Wuest's translation because he appropriately uses "ruin" for "destroy"
in this verse. Destroy implies annihilation to non-being which is contrary to the very point
I'm trying to make and that I believe is taught in the Bible. Occasionally soul is used to
mean one's life in the sense of one's living process, livelihood, or lifestyle. This is like when
Jesus is characterized as the Good Shepard depicting the character of His personality in
His lifestyle. He gave His *pneuma*/spirit/life for the sheep when He physically died on the
cross. He gave the whole of His living process (soul) to and/or for the sheep when He died
to Himself by doing nothing the Father did not tell or give Him to do. He lived for thirty-three plus years without sinning one time, though "tempted in all wise such as ye and me"
(Heb.4:15). In His own humanness "such as ye and me," He performed the same identical
bio-psycho-socio-politico-culturalo-spiritual dynamics that you and I contend with, i.e.,
the same spiritual warfare. He gave His soul, in the sense of lifestyle, for the benefit of the
sheep as He totally died to Self (soul) in the performance of His own humanity with total
obedience to "my Father and my God, and your Father and your God" (Jn.20:17). As the
Good Shepherd, Jesus gave His life in every way for us, His sheep. He did for me and you
that which you and I cannot do for ourselves, essentially overcome sin and its wages of death
and, if unredeemed, resurrected to damnation, if redeemed, resurrected to life (Jn.5:29).
Thank God for the hope of an abundant, prosperous, final outcome.

[34] (From *The New Testament: An Expanded Translation* by Kenneth S. Wuest Copyright ©
1961 by Wm. B. Eerdmans Publishing Co. All rights reserved.)

[35] "In the beginning was the Word, and the Word was with God, and the Word was God. He
[the Word] was in the beginning with God. All things were made through Him [the Word],
and without Him [the Word] nothing was made that was made. In Him [the Word] was life,
and the life was the light of men. And the light shines in the darkness, and the darkness did
not comprehend it. He [the Word] was in the world, and the world was made through Him,
and the world did not know Him. But as many as received Him, to them He [the Word]
gave the right to become children of God, to those who believe in His [the Word's] name:
who [those who believed in His name] were born, *not* of blood, *nor* of the will of the flesh,
nor of the will of man, *but* [were re-born or regenerated] of God. And the Word became
flesh and dwelt among us, and we beheld His glory, the glory as of the only begotten of the
Father, full of grace and truth" (John 1:1-14 NKJV emphasis added).

body biologically alive (including the brain) or makes the body have life in it. It likewise is the energetic, vitalizing, property, element, or means of "life-itizing" the soul.

Eternality is also inherent in the soul, that other component of which our being made in God's image consists. As all the characteristics of God's nature — like love, power, righteousness, and holiness — are identifiably different but inseparable in God's nature, so are the characteristics of His being Spirit and having a soul (the characteristics with which we are created in His image) identifiably different but inseparable. They, in fact, "come in" together when we are conceived and they "go out" together when we die.

They are the vehicle, the filtering system through which the relationship between God and each of us is modulated. The negative factors affecting the outcome of this process are the materialistic socio-politico-cultural influence of the world, the sinful bent of my own worldly flesh, and Satan, the enemy General of the invisible warfare going on in and for our very spirits, souls, and bodies. The wholeness of the epitome of God's creation — man — is the (mine and your) spirit, soul, and body for which Paul prayed saying, "Now may the God of peace Himself sanctify you completely; and may your whole spirit, soul, and body be preserved blameless at the coming of our Lord Jesus Christ."[36]

What follows in this book is an attempt to describe, usefully, warring factors' contributing influence to its outcome factors regarding the interaction of the nature of the spirit and soul

---

[36] 1 Thessalonians 5:23 (NKJV)

relationship — as manifested by physical behavior of the body and the choices decided on for the body to carry out.

Spirit (life) and soul (mind) are identifiably different but inseparable – that which makes us alive and that which makes us consciously aware of it. The spirit and soul irrevocably include the unlimitedness of eternality. Eternality is a qualitative characteristic of our being created in God's image. God is eternal, the "Great I AM." The functional interaction of the Holy Spirit in our regenerated spirit, informs, reminds and, thereby, empowers our soul/mind to be spiritually minded in our decisions (choices).

It is vital to note here that God has no brain, but He has Personhood and personality, as He has given us and, through this "vehicle," we have a relationship with Him. With this Scripturally-founded understanding now, God has just clarified that that part of us created in His image is **not** that which we erroneously, unrealistically and, therein, unhealthfully most commonly think of **as ourselves**, i.e, our bodies —- that could not possibly be an accurate truth because God declares unequivocally He is Spirit! (John 4:24 KJV)

Considering thoughtfully further, can you or anyone you know on the face of this earth hand me a pound of spirit or "life," per se? Can you weigh and measure it out for me or yourself? Conjointly can you hand me a pound of thought, feeling, attitude, intelligence, judgment or intellectual activity? To every question the answer is a resounding, "NO! NOT POSSIBLE!"

So, that part of us that is created in the image of God does not include the body, because, again, **God doesn't have a body**.

God is Spirit and has a Soul.
He does not have a body.

The qualitative characteristic in which God's image consists in us, then, is the immaterial, non-physical aspects of ourselves – our spirit and soul – the life in us, and the mind faculty for cognition, reasoning, and **choice-making**.

Biblical Language

In John 6:63 Jesus said, "The words I have spoken to you are Spirit, and life" (CJB). John 4:24 says, "God is spirit" (KJV). Genesis 2:7 says, "God formed man of the dust of the ground, and breathed (Spirited) into his nostrils the breath (spirit) of life; and man became a living "soul" (KJV), or "being" (NIV), or "person" (NLT). We talked about the lexical correlation of the words breath and spirit and here we find further relevance of the correlation in the language of the Bible. The practical value of recognizing the correlation is that it can help us more readily understand the use of these terms in Scripture. Then we are able to transpose their message into our secular environment with more wisely **chosen behavior** because of the more accurate spiritual understanding for cultivating the healthiest (being my own best friend vs. being my own worst enemy) practical application of the meaning of the term used. "The truth/reality will make you free" (John 8:32 Emphasis added).

Spirit (Distinguished from Soul)

We can now consider the spirit a little further. Spirit is the life. When it was put (breathed) into the dead dirt, the dirt became the living body. The Spirit quality of God's character that He imparted to man as life inherently carries the energetic, fueling element of God's Creative Power (EGP) with it. It never is a part of man himself, but is at some level of his psycho-spiritual functioning in his awareness.[37] In addition, it is available to his earthly life for the asking and is expressed in the eternality of his being, irrelevant to himself, and purely as an expression of the EGP quality of his Creator's character and nature.

Also, let's look closer at the Greek word *pneuma* translated by the English word "spirit" in its equivalence as "life." James 2:26 explains, "As the body without the spirit is dead, so faith without works is dead also" (KJV). Not a single translation, of which I use thirty-three regularly, says "As the body is dead without the soul..." Additionally, John 19:30 states that just before dying on the cross —- being dead, without having "life" in His body any longer —- "...He [Jesus] said, 'It is finished, and gave up His spirit!'" That is, He died, His body "without the spirit" was dead. He no longer had *pneuma*, spirit, or life in His body. Not a single translation uses the word soul there.

---

[37] There's never been a culture, no matter how primitive, that did not have a religious expression.

The Lord Ain't Just Whistling Dixie

However, these statements regarding Biblical language are certainly consistent with God's Word where He declares unequivocally that the spirit and soul are not the same. In 1 Thessalonians 5:23, Paul says, "I pray your whole spirit, soul, and body be preserved until the coming of that day (of Jesus' return)." Hebrews 4:12 repeats, "For the word of God is quick, and powerful, and sharper than any two-edged sword, **piercing even to dividing asunder of soul and spirit,** and of the joints and marrow..." (emphasis added). The intended understanding which God repeated the same way twice needs no further translation, because the Lord "ain't just whistling Dixie." Not one translation includes the word "and" nor has a comma between the three words: spirit, soul, and body. **The spirit and the soul are not the same.** *They are inseparable, but not the same.* Likewise, the body is a separate material mass which was caused to become alive by the imbuement of Spirit (life) into it and, simultaneously, imbued with the capacity to think, sense, emote, judge, and choose (or exercise) will. **Personhood** was established. The material mass was now the *soma* or body, and the components of man's total personality were complete as clearly identified by the Lord in the two Scriptures cited above: his spirit, *pneuma*; his soul, *psuche*; and his body, *soma* as stated in the Greek.

In His own purpose, God first created the material, physical universe —- the world. He then created creatures to be in the environmental context of the universe or the world. He just **spoke** them into being! According to what He has told us, He finished

His creation activity with the epitome of His desired and chosen creation purposes, man, putting something of Himself into man that set us apart from all the other creatures. Because of the nature of the life or spirit He put in us, and the soul that comes with it, we have an awareness of God and, in that, an awareness **of** Him in relation **to** us (Who's who), along with an awareness of Him in relationship **with** us (the mercy of His grace).

Life

So, here we will understand that God is Spirit. Yes, He put some of His non-created Self into the non-living dead dirt He'd previously created and formed it into the shape of our bodies. As a result, that non-living dead material immediately became alive with all the physiology, epigenetics, enzymes, and neurotransmitters all in place and operant because it now had some elements of God's nature in it that thus instilled its inherent vitally "energized" significance, meaning, and purpose. It now had spirit, or **life**, in it —- but, specifically relevant to our work here, it had more than that. It also had another quality that seems to be inherent in Spirit and, though not the same, it seems, according to God's Word, to be inseparable. That is, when God put some of His non-created Self into the formed dirt, He not only put Spirit or Life into that physical mass, He also concomitantly put **soul** into it and it became a **living soul, being, person** —- a man (see Scriptural reference opening this section).

The Soul and the Mind

We need to understand that God not only **is** Spirit, but immanent in His spiritual nature is also soul or personhood. If there is life, there is some degree of individuated personhood or personality. There is intelligence, judgement, and choice-making, influenced by cohabiting emotions which presages the exercise of will. Reasonably, then, this correlates soul with *mind*. In fact, the Greek word for soul is *psuche* from which we get our English word *psyche* or psychology, i.e., mental activity.

We need to understand, too, in the sense of man being able to think, to experience and express emotional feelings and adopt attitudes —- all components of our personhood —- that God not only *is* Spirit, He also *has* a (S)oul. He thinks and has emotions. "I know the thoughts that I have toward you, saith the Lord, thoughts of peace, and not of evil, to give you a future and hope" (Jeremiah 29:11 NKJV). "'For My thoughts are not your thoughts, neither are your ways My ways,' says the Lord" (Isaiah 55:8 NKJV). "The New Moons and your appointed feasts My soul hates" (Isaiah 1:14 NKJV). "I will set My tabernacle among you, and My soul will not abhor you" (Leviticus 36:11 NKJV).

We will rely heavily on these biblically-based understandings as we seek to grasp some things the Lord would have us comprehend for the purpose of translating the supernatural into the natural or, more accurately, to bring the natural into the truth of its correlation with the supernatural and apply the correlation in our everyday living experience.

Supernatural Science and Natural Science

This Biblical language seems to be the Scriptural supportive corroboration that the spirit is what energizes, fuels, and empowers what we call our biology. Biology refers to cellular bio-chemistry, physiology, enzymes, hormones, and neurophysiology, including the neurotransmitters of the brain.

From their atheistic perspective, each of these described activities is actually no more than exactly what the materialists claim them to be, simply chemical reactions. They would say there's no greater significance to what's happening in your liver and brain than what's taking place in the rest of the material "realm," even out into however far the universe(s) go. They would say it's all the same—just chemistry! The more informed would say it's just the physics of quantum mechanics which seems to be more and more accepted as the "stuff" of what "chemistry" is all about.

They can't account for the obvious difference between the "physical" chemistry taking place in the "being" of a rock and the "bio" chemistry taking place in the "being" of a human. They not only don't know what that difference is, but from whence it came or why, yet they have "faith" in what they "know" it's not—and that's God! However, I have observed that the more quantum physics is studied and understood, the greater the number of unbiased scientists who are coming to the conclusion that if one follows the evidence it points to, if not the biblically Judeo-Christian God, at least to some "Intelligence" supporting what is being recognized as design and purpose in the materiality of the world (universe).

However, the "biology" did not exist until God breathed His *pneuma* spirit into and infused some of His qualitative characteristics of His own non-created Self into the not-alive matter, the dead, non-sensing, non-thinking, non-emoting, purely chemically interactive material. Thus and then, the material so infused was imbued with the super-material, super-natural "Charge" of life and mind, i.e., **spirit** and **soul**. Only then, **with the complete system of physiology and biochemistry in place functionally**, did the material (dirt) itself become the *soma*, the body. The biology of the *soma* wasn't there without the *pneuma* and *psuche*. When the *pneuma* and *psuche* leave the *soma* the biological systems are no longer operative and the *soma* returns to what it was before, just dead dirt. It conforms according to the Second Law of Thermodynamics. All matter is subject to entropy. It decays. In its most simple conceptualization, we can infer that there is no qualitative property inherent in any form of matter to cause, or even account for, the phenomenon we observe to be and call life.

It would seem very reasonable then to consider that what (or Who) ever caused the "life" to be in any form of "living" matter also caused the matter itself to be. And that's exactly what God's Word declares to us at John 1:1-14.

Moreover, as will later be discussed about how all this is also not only relevant to death, but in addition how it contributes to increased exercising of faith in our "everyday living experience" or our "psychology." Or, seen from another perspective, "recognizing and dealing with so much of what our daily living process seems to be involved with – and that's *spiritual warfare!*" Remember, God ain't stupid and He ain't impractical and, as most of us desire, we are to be doers of His – most of us desire to be doers of the Word, not hearers only. Remember, also, that's what this book is all about.

Also inherent in each of us in this dynamic is the very human, self-centered thought that, "I want what I want, right when I want it, just because I want it, and since it's me that wants it, I have a right to it!" The reality of this is easily demonstrated. Put two toddlers on the floor. Give one 49 toys and the other one. The one with the 49 will not have played with half of those he has before he wants the one toy the other has. He wants it ALL! Every one of us comes here with that. We do not want to be limited in any way or to any degree. This dynamic is the Sin Nature. The psychological term is Narcissism. Remember Narcissus? Remember how Lucifer became Satan? (Jn.1:3 KJV).

The Actuality of the Reality of Immateriality

Perhaps the most hopeful, intellectually satisfying, and pragmatically reasonable basis upon which to exercise the conduction of one's "Life" in its living process would be, at the least, congruent with the reasoning of Pascal's Wager.

Blaise Pascal, a French philosopher and mathematician, raised a religio-philosophical question known as Pascal's Wager. It concerns some of our inquiry here. In its simplest form it considers, "If God exists, what is the consequent risk value to live your life based on the denial of His existence vs. if God does not exist, what is the consequent value gained in being right about it and living your life accordingly?"[38] Simply put, if your position is He doesn't exist, and you're right that He doesn't exist, then you've gained 70-75 years of doing only what was pleasurable to you personally. If you're wrong in that position, you wagered for 70-75 years of pleasure against constant, unrelenting non-pleasure, against an unimaginable **eternity** of unrelenting suffering and misery, **and are lost** with no hope of relief! Pascal was appealing to man's capacity for logic. The most naive bettor would reject those odds on purely intelligent logic. Moreover, as I say, "God ain't stupid and He ain't impractical." The notion of winning Pascal's Wager is based on a wishful and unrealistic belief in magic. In that vein, Jesus said, "If you can't believe what I'm saying to you, at least believe because of the works (miracles) **you see me do**" (John 10:38 emphasis added). In other words, use your head. Learn from experience.

One goal of this book is to bring the reader to the **recognition of the actuality of the reality of immateriality!** The spirit and soul, the life and mind, are of the immaterial realm. The body, including the brain, is of the material realm. This seems a good place to clearly substantiate my earlier declaration that the brain in not the mind.

---

[38] Blaise Pascal

The Brain Is Not the Mind

"If it is for mind that we are searching the brain, then we are supposing the brain to be much more than a telephone-exchange. We are supposing it to be a telephone-exchange along with subscribers as well."
-Charles Scott Sherrington, Nobel Prize-winning neuroscientist

Materialists want to consider the brain merely as a computer. Software pioneer Bill Gates is quoted to have said, "I don't think there's anything unique about human intelligence. All the neurons in the brain that make up perceptions and emotions operate in a binary fashion."[39] Artificial intelligence guru Marvin Minsky said, "The human mind is a computer made out of meat."[40] At the end of the twentieth century, philosopher of the mind, John Searle and others "were convinced that a computer that thinks like a human being was quite possible. After all, the human brain was thought to *be* a computer." Ray Curzwell, author of "The Age of Spiritual Machines," said, "Supercomputers will achieve one human brain capacity by 2010, a personal computer will do so by about 2020.... By the 2030s, the non-biological portion of our intelligence will predominate."[41]

---

[39] The Spiritual Brain; Mario Beauregard & Denyse O'Leary; Harper One; 2008; pg. 23

[40] Ibid.

[41] pg.19 Beauregard, Spiritual Brain

In 1952, artificial intelligence (AI) pioneer Alan Turing wrote the first computer chess program. In 1980, a $100,000 award was offered to any software programmer who could build a computer that could beat any chess player such as the Russian grand master Garry Kasparov. In 1996, after saying "Machines are stupid by nature," Kasparov notoriously beat the most powerful computer built at that time, IBM's Deep Blue. However, in 1997, he just as notoriously lost to Deep Blue. The programmers were awarded their prize and the age of the spiritual machine was about to begin. Carl Sagan, renowned astronomer, astrophysicist, and astrobiologist said, "Because of a kind of human chauvinism or anthropocentrism, many humans are reluctant to admit this possibility. But I think it is inevitable."[42]

The age of the spiritual machine went by so fast that practically everyone missed it. In 2003, Kasparov tied the much more powerful Deep Junior and another program, X3dFritz. Deep Junior powered through up to 3 million possible moves per second. Kasparov probably evaluated only two to three moves per second.[43] This raises obvious questions: Why does Kasparov *ever* win? Shouldn't he always lose? Philosopher and chess

---

[42] Carl Sagan, who also had a public persona, died in 1966. Appearing on The Johnny Carson Show he affirmed he had terminal cancer with not long to live. Carson asked his thoughts about death, dying, and faith. He stated he was jealous of those who have faith and wished that he could, and then stated, "but my intelligence just won't let me!" Beginning with how and why Lucifer became Satan (Isa.14), to Eve and Adam, and even unto today, we humans have had a problem with the sense of our own capacity to "know" and through that to effectuate our own desired ultimate and final outcome. As if we even could conceive of or cause a more "prosperous and abundant" outcome for ourselves than can the One Who *is all that is POWER*, God. Remember Narcissus!

[43] Mario Beauregard & Denyse O'Leary; *The Spiritual Brain,* "Harper One" 2008; pg. 22

enthusiast, Tim McGrew, put it: "Something is going on in the grand master's mind that is not only radically different ... but also inconceivably more efficient."[44]

Computers don't form or follow plans, nor do they have goals. They don't have overarching ideas, nor use analogy or metaphors. They don't have any sense of value of winning or losing, accomplishing or failing. What they do is perform calculations. Computer pioneer John Holland pointed out, "There are many artificial intelligence problems that cannot be solved by simply performing more calculations."[45] John Searle described the early optimistic ideas about AI as "hopelessly mistaken."[46]

So, the human brain is not a calculating machine, and a calculating machine cannot answer our questions about the meaning of life. Computers, however cleverly we human beings build them, do not become spiritual machines, nor can they shed light on the spirit (life bearing) or soul (thinking, emoting, judging, and will exercising) aspects of the nature of humans.

Look, think, and consider this with me: You could hand me a pound of brain, could you not? Not your own, but you can measure out a pound of brain and hand it to me. But can you hand me a pound of mind? That's not an option to do because it is not material, not matter. It cannot be weighed or measured. The behaviorist and other materialists would say "...if you can't

---

[44] Ibid, pg. 22

[45] John Holland, *The Virginia Engineer*, Circle C. Corporation, 2003; Vol. 52, pg. 16

[46] John Searle, *The Spiritual Brain*; Mario Beauregard & Denyse O'Leary; Harper One; 2008; pg. 23

weigh or measure it, it isn't real." That can't make sense because, right now, as you read this something is happening between you and me. There is no physicality involved directly though. I made these physical marks we call letters at some point in time and, through your eyeballs' biochemical and neurophysiological function of transmitting light impulses to your brain, it is recording them. However, the brain, per se, knows nothing about translating or interpreting any meaning, intention, or purpose inherent in the marks.

If the brain were the mind, the brain of someone who never saw English before could read what you're reading. It could translate and interpret it. Someone who has only seen (read) Japanese "marks" before could also read these English "marks" if the brain, per se, is from whence the translation and understanding come. But that's not reality or truth. To someone who can only read (translate and interpret) Japanese, they would only see these markings as random scratching on a piece of paper with no meaning.

The Mind Is a Function of the Brain

So, then, we are to understand that the brain is not the mind, but the mind is **a** function **of** the brain as a physical organ. To grasp the full significance of this, however, we must also understand how **immeasurably different the activity** of the **sub**atomic particles that make up the physical atomic particles that make up the molecular particles that make up the cells, and then tissues, that are then organized into what we call organs which then cooperatively interact with one another in a purely physical system we call the body, the *soma*. In one sense, the interaction occurring in, between, and among the body organs we call the liver, kidneys, and thyroid gland is at the most primary level no more than "electrochemical chemical activity" of the same nature taking place at the particle level of which they consist and interact. Only at that level we talk about nano-quantum organization of physics, while at this higher level of macro organization we talk medically about physiology.

According to the most recent science earlier noted, all this physical material has as its most basic particle the Higgs boson – called by some "the God particle" because it is what gives any material thing its mass and is the matrix within which all other matter is dependent upon for its contextual existence. All of this produces observable results just as occurred in Cern, Switzerland in the six-mile-long Large Hadron Collider when this "God particle," the Higgs boson, was observed. Now we have to remember that the Higgs boson is only a **form of energy**. Some of its properties, a primary one of which is its extremely rapid decay, have made it so difficult for scientists to demonstrate. At this point, the Higgs boson is believed to fill space and "create" (my term) a matrix, the Higgs Field, within which all other matter "resides." The interaction of these other particles with the Higgs boson "excites" the field in such a way as to result in some of them acquiring the character of mass.

Now to reach the goal of what I'm trying to help the reader understand, and without the desire, intent, expertise, or need to get any further into quantum mechanics, let me state that all matter is a form of mass. Mass is the *M value* in Einstein's equation E=mc2. Transliterated it says Energy (that level of the Higgs boson which is at this point believed to fill space and "create" (my term) a matrix) and mass are essentially equivalent.

The result of the myriads of "processes" of which this action (from the sub-microscopic nano-quantum physical size of matter all the way up to the macro size of the matter observed as the physical organs of the human body) consists is what produces the liver "**function**," kidney "**function**," and the thyroid "**function**." That's no more than what is taking place in the body's organ we call the brain. The liver, kidneys, thyroid, and brain all operate on the same identical principles underlying every chemical reaction. Chemical reactions are based on "energy," whatever that is.

We humans obviously don't know because we didn't make it and can't cause it "to be," (i.e., can't create "it"), nor can we destroy it. We don't know of what energy per se consists. We can demonstrate that it exists because we see the results of its **functional** operations just as we know the mind exists. Even though it is immaterial, the actuality of its reality is continually demonstrated evidentially as a **function** of the brain just as readily understood as the **function** the other organs.

Is it our greatest "brains," as it sometimes is stated colloquially, or our most intelligent "minds" that tell us $E=mc^2$? The materialists among them agree that matter is just differently configured forms of energy. I have no quarrel with that. In fact, I agree. But, I am led to an entirely different logical, intellectually reasonable, and compelling point of consideration than that of the materialist. It stems from the significance of not knowing what energy is or "from where did it come, and/or why does it exist in the first place."

So, then, the brain is not the mind nor is the mind the brain. *The mind, however is a function OF the brain. But only as long as whatever the "I" of "me" is (whatever that is), is in the body!* The differentiating question "What is the 'I' of 'me'?" is very much like "is the brain the mind or perhaps vice versa?" The answer is what we are trying to conceive of though and is, also, conceptually outside our bounds to do so – it is in the realm of **"something more"** spoken of earlier. It is the phenomenal experience of revelation! It's like an enigma in the context of a conundrum. However, God ain't stupid and He ain't impractical. Nor is He, as we not infrequently hear, "a God of confusion." His Word is not given to us for confusion, but to deepen our understanding so we can be more Spiritually-minded and, in that, be able to perform more obedience which is the sacrifice He most desires because it is the manifestation of faith.

D6

Faith comes from
HEARING THE WORD

★ Clarifying **"NOUS,"** the Greek
word for the mental activity for
the process of understanding
and deriving choice.

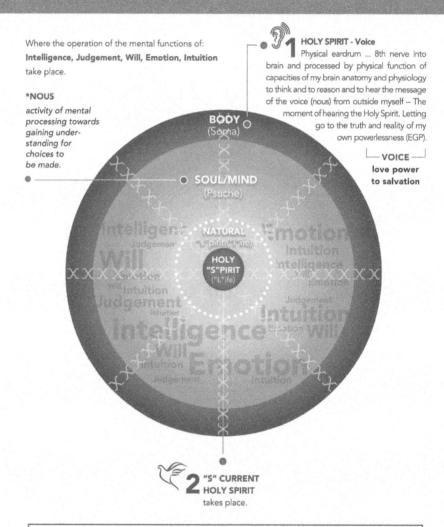

Where the operation of the mental functions of:
Intelligence, Judgement, Will, Emotion, Intuition
take place.

*NOUS

*activity of mental
processing towards
gaining under-
standing for
choices to
be made.*

HOLY SPIRIT - Voice
Physical eardrum ... 8th nerve into
brain and processed by physical function of
capacities of my brain anatomy and physiology
to think and to reason and to hear the message
of the voice (nous) from outside myself – The
moment of hearing the Holy Spirit. Letting
go to the truth and reality of my
own powerlessness (EGP).

└─ **VOICE** ─┘
**love power
to salvation**

BODY
(Soma)

SOUL/MIND
(Psuche)

NATURAL
"s"pirit ("L"ife)

**HOLY
"S"PIRIT**
("L"ife)

Intelligence
Judgement
Will
Emotion
Intuition
Will
Intuition
Judgement
Intuition
Intelligence
Will
Intuition
Judgement
Emotion
Intuition
Intelligence
Emotion
Judgement
Intuition
Emotion
Will

**2 "S" CURRENT
HOLY SPIRIT**
takes place.

Jesus said, "My words (immaterial) are Spirit (immaterial) ..."[John 6:63] – The words
[NOISE] are not the information --- the words convey the information which is the
message (immaterial). So, there is no way materialists can weigh or measure
immaterial reality and this limits their sciences. The brain is not the mind nor is
the mind the brain, but the mind is a function of the brain.

The Spirit Informs the Soul/Mind

The spirit energizes, enlivens, or puts literal life into the soul, as it were (See diagram D6, page 98). As Johannes I. Marais expressed it in his article on "Mind" in the International Bible Encyclopedia regarding 2 Timothy 2:7, "The Lord give thee understanding (*sunesis*) in all things" (KJV emphasis added). That is to say, as he further expresses it, "An understanding **enlightened from above!**" (emphasis added). That is an **enlightened**, grasping, comprehensively **revealed understanding** from Heaven by the Holy Spirit from God Himself. We're speaking here of a scope of understanding that is so far removed from mere human intellect that to speak of it in the same context is almost blasphemous.

The magnitude of the dramatic difference between the **natural** spirit and the **regenerated** spirit must be clearly understood here also. Though the natural spirit is the life in the body, the natural spirit is dead to God. The oneness in the relationship with God in the beginning was lost, separated, in trespass. Yes, the natural spirit is the energic, in-fueling life essence in the person, so the person is alive in his natural biological life. However, since the Garden Fall, all natural, un-regenerated human spirit life is dead to God. Ephesians 2:1 says, "And you hath He quickened, who were dead in trespasses and sins." Ephesians 2:4-5 says, "But God...even when we were dead in sins (i.e., our spirits having been separated from the **living** God), hath quickened us...." Being separated from the EGP of God's Holy Spirit and not having the saving redemptive **relationship** provided in that Yahweh-Elohim

All Loving Power — which *is* God — man is left with just his natural material body, and only his natural materialistic frame of reference to inform his natural soul or mind! That is to say, when Jesus' "here-now" representative, the Holy Spirit, comes into a person's spirit, and is thereby regenerated, the Holy Spirit is then present in his spirit and **informs the soul or mind.** 1 Corinthians. 5:9-10 explicates it thusly, "**But God hath revealed [the things of God] to us by His Spirit**" (emphasis added).

So, the **spirit informs the soul.** It vitalizes our soul/mind for the expression and manifestation of our invisible individuated personhood **through** the body, which part is not made in the image of God because it is material and, in that sense, is of this world (See again diagram D6, page 98; See diagrams D7 and D7a, pages 101-102). The two invisible, non-material components of our personality are expressed and demonstrate their presence and reality, if you will, by and through their use of the third component of the total personality structure, that of the physical, material component—the body. A familiar comparative analogy is that one wouldn't know the wind existed if you didn't experience the curtain's movement.

○ Where the operation of the mental functions of:

Intelligence, Judgement, Will, Emotion, Intuition

take place

To understand this diagram clearly, you must realize that the soul and spirit are separately identifiable but are literally inseparable. Life and nous (or soul/mind) activity always exist together. Other Scriptures clarify this even further.

JOB 32:8

But it is the spirit in man, the breath of the Almighty, that makes him understand.

1 COR 2:14

The person without the Spirit does not accept the things that come from the Spirit of God but considers them foolishness, and cannot understand them because they are discerned only through the Spirit.

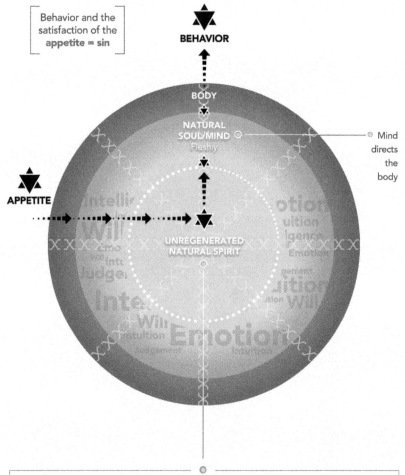

Behavior and the
satisfaction of the
appetite = sin

BEHAVIOR

BODY

NATURAL
SOUL/MIND
Fleshly

Mind
directs
the
body

APPETITE

UNREGENERATED
NATURAL SPIRIT

REMINDER

Again, note that the natural spirit has nothing of value to offer the soul/mind
because each is as fleshly as the other as depicted by the "x's" in Diagrams 3-5

One of the main goals of this work is to develop a deeper and broader understanding of the significance, or the lack thereof, of ourselves in relation **to** God. Our discussion of the spirit informing the soul will enhance this understanding.

I also desire to enhance the scope of awareness and understanding of His merciful grace towards us by having a relationship **with** us and, in that, allowing us to be in a relationship **with** Him.

This work is an effort to help us humans to personalize our relationship with the Triune Divine Source in such a way as to not interfere with the Holy Spirit's desire and function to effectuate a deeper, more committed relationship with Elohim-Yahweh through God the Son. It behooves us, in gratitude, to remember that everything in our relationship **with** God is **towards** us from Him *first!* "We love Him because He first loved us" (1 John 4:19 NKJV). The **first** is the merciful grace of the Agape Love of God the Father. Though He "...was tempted in all wise such as thee and me..." (Hebrews 4:15), the Son of man —- God the Son —- **performed perfectly** (sinless) right in the midst of and through the totally identified-with-us biopsychospiritual dynamics of His fully **human personhood** —- specifically including His body —- and, through this, providing us the relationship-effectuating EGP of God the Holy Spirit (See again diagrams D6, page 98; D7 and D7a, pages 101-102).

Understanding God Power

Any discipline, be it education, philosophy, theology, or science, forfeits its claim to Christian legitimacy when it:

(1) Questions or denies the Deity of Jesus, the Logos Word, the I AM before the cosmos or **matter** was–the Christ! (John 1:1

(2) Their skull and bones, true colors of apostasy unfurl when they question or deny His virgin birth.

(3) His sinless **performance** of life (the same Life "Spirited" into Adam who failed such performance) manifested **in the material form of flesh**, having to **exercise faith** daily and executing the power of choice to freely submit His will, **or not**, amidst every human temptation for *thirty-three plus years*.

(4) Question or deny His miracles, qua **miracles** (acts only the Elohim Creator God can do) rather than some natural phenomenon which is to be explained or replicated by science.

(5) Question or deny that, though sinless (Hebrews 4:15), therefore not even subject to death (neither physical material–first death, nor spiritual–second death: Romans 6:23, Revelation 20:5-6), He **experienced** the biopsychospiritual dynamical processing, and innocent acceptance of the penalty of death within His then **fully human** tripartite structural personality (1 Thessalonians 5:23 and Hebrews 4:12); thus provided justification before the Father, and therein redemption, for every man who **chooses to receive** it.

(6) Question or deny that it was an actual physical death and bodily, though Spiritual bodily, resurrection three days later. (1 Corinthians 5:44)

The greater more subtle negative significance sub-serving each of these stances is the implicit denial of the "all POWER-ness" of God (Psalm 62:11). We intellectually acknowledge this all Power-ness God characteristic with the word Omnipotence. However, as I intend to clarify, this term does not effectually convey the emotional, experiential reality of what it desires to communicate and why it would **seem so necessary** for humankind to attempt to negate the literal **reality** of the miraculous Elohim God Power (EGP) events enumerated above. It will become logically comprehensible why their being miracles is the very reason it is believingly **felt** they must be not only denied but, literally, negated.

These **most fundamental premises to Christianity** are the most offensive and defense-provoking to non-believers and apostates. Since these premises cannot be refuted and to avoid their soteriology being believed and understood as relevant to today's culture, those offended by these biblically Christian premises seem defensively motivated to at least keep the Truth busy apologetically by a contrary literature presenting conclusions derived from "reasonably unquestionable facts."[47]

---

[47] Robert Jastrow and Norman Podhoretz substantiate this statement in their discussion entitled, "Two Faces of Reality"; *The Marshall Institute*; http://www.marshall.org/article.php?id=60 (Dec. 12, 2000): "...it is not a matter of another year, another decade of work, another measurement, or another theory; at this moment it seems as though science will never be able to raise the curtain on the mystery of creation." (p. 9).

But it is rife with inconclusive speculative assumptions or presuppositions, regardless of inaccurate application of pieces of Truth employed in humanistic or other naturalistic "no God of the gaps" worldviews. If their academic, scientific, and/or theology positions cannot confute the Truth, then their answers to man's question of his origin and ultimate state of being are left vulnerable to observed, objective Truth that man knows not even what **power** is. In that sense, they remain challenged by pragmatic experience and a reality that man's highest, most technical science cannot even initiate much less replicate! In our separated-from-Completeness sin state, such a simple, **complete** and **ultimate Truth** irresistibly crushes the self-perpetuated lie, that man can provide **security** for himself. This cherished lie, no matter the form presented to himself, and erroneously believing he must, perpetuates his clinging tenaciously to it in a **desperately organized chaos** which is recognized clinically in his **symptoms** and **maladaptive lifestyles**. Paradoxically, the Truth that "**power** belongs to God,"[48] so fearfully defended against, is the very thing God promises will set us free!

In ancient times, names often reflect the bearer's personal traits and characteristics. This ancient cultural practice serves us well here. Gary Hedrick wrote a series of articles on The Hebrew Names of God. The first article was right to our point:

---

[48] Ps. 62:11 (Twenty-one of twenty-six versions translate Strong's 5797 as power rather than strength).

"The ancient sages of Israel said that the name *Elohim* denotes God's power, judgment, and severity, while the name YHVH [Yahweh, Jehovah] points to His mercy and leniency (Genesis Rabbah XXXIII.3).

They noted that these two *names—Elohim* and YHVH—often appear together.

The English Bible translates the YHVH Elohim as 'LORD God,' thus emphasizing both His mercy, love, and leniency (YHVH), *and* His power, judgment, and severity *(Elohim)*."[49]

Hedrick further points out that Elohim is the masculine, plural of the root word *el* meaning God generically. That God refers to Himself in the masculine sense is not only relevant in today's confused socio-culturally politically correct atmosphere (and in some Bible "translator's" understanding), but even more relevant is that He uses the plural to include the Triune Oneness of Himself. "In the beginning God created (*Elohim* created)." It must most certainly be pertinent that this descriptive name is used at the very beginning – at the Creation. As we tend to do **by our nature** and are being more and more **subversively taught** from elementary school into graduate and post-graduate education, we think in the narrowed view of the laws of Physics: we think of the **force** of a nuclear explosion as a means of measuring

---

49 Gary Hedrick, "The Hebrew Names of God, Part 1," *Message of the Christian Jew* (The Christian Jew Foundation, January-February 1996), 6.

"power" and of **energy** in the physical sense as "power" required for the creation of the universe and all that's in it. Then, Hedrick points out, "No wonder the Holy Spirit prompted Moses to use *Elohim,* the name that emphasizes God's power, in the opening verse of the Creation account."[50] Moreover, we can also begin to understand, "The name **Elohim, then, prepares the way for the <u>fuller revelation of the Godhead</u> in the rest of Scripture**[51] (emphasis added).

Others concur, but Grundmann in Kittel's *Theological Dictionary of the New Testament,* Vol. 2, states it succinctly:

> "The supremacy of God as the Creator and Lord of the world is maintained in Judaism — and ***the essence of God is found in His power.*** As the name of God retreats into the background in Judaism, being replaced by paraphrases, one of these descriptions is "power." Jesus uses this before the Sanhedrin – (Mt.26:64; Mk. 14:62) — [Also in the Targums] when God speaks of Himself in the first person, "power" is again one of the terms used — e.g., Tg. 0. Dt. 33:26 — There is here no [personification] of the concept of power but a paraphrase of the name of God and the ***divine I.*** The fact that the concept of power could be used in

---

[50] Gary Hedrick, "The Hebrew Names of God, Part 1," *Message of the Christian Jew* (The Christian Jew Foundation, January-February 1996), 6.

[51] Ibid.

this way shows us to what extent **the essence of God consists in His power** according to the view of Judaism"[52] (emphasis added).

Finally, I can crystallize the specific point I'm trying to get across here. As noted previously, everything rests on and follows or develops out of this **cornerstone premise**; all that **power** actually is (and we mere creature humans do not and cannot really know what that is) belongs to God. As the pre-eminent atheistic philosopher, Anthony Flew, declared, honoring his lifelong credo of following the evidence, "There is a God Who is outside this physical universe, beyond the limited realm of inquiry of mere science."[53, 54] Again Grundmann has stated it as clearly as I have found by a Biblical scholar:

> "To the righteousness and holiness of God we should add His glory, the manifestation, recognition, revelation and magnifying of which are *effected by His power*"[55] (emphasis added).

It is **this effectual** aspect that makes **all** the difference. Without the Elohim-Power characteristic of God, the Yahweh-Love characteristic could hold no more promise or hope of

[52] Grundmann, "Ideas of Power in Rabbinical and Hellenistic Judaism," *Theological Dictionary of the New Testament*, Vol. 2, Ed. Kittel (Grand Rapids, MI: Eerdmans, 1964), 297.

[53] Antony Flew; *There Is No A God* HarperOne; 2007

[54] Op. Cit., Jastrow & Podhoretz.

[55] Op. Cit., Grundmann, 293.

security than any other god because it could not be **effectuated!** And, remember, trying to overcome the reality of our vulnerability and striving for **security** is what we in our physical, biological bodies are all about. *Without even realizing it, the bottom line motivation within us, regardless of the form in which it is expressed, is toward gaining* **absolute security or immortality.**

In each person, the bottom line motivation is gaining absolute security or immortality.

Remember, for everything having life in it the ultimate pain is the pain of *death*. We desire immortality. We desire invulnerability to *death*. We fear *death* above all things. We can, and many do, deny this. Like all other Truth, however, Reality doesn't change because *I* deny the fact of it. We, as well-informed and educated professionals and clinicians (especially), ought to be able to relate to this human characteristic. Moreover, God tells this about ourselves in Hebrews 2:15, "And deliver them who through fear of death were *all* their lifetime subject to bondage." (KJV emphasis added).

From before the time we are born, our behavior is influenced by an awareness within ourselves that our biology could stop "ticking" at any moment, and we are **powerless** to do anything about it!

God says we are in bondage **because** of the fear of **death.** This is where the **Yahweh-Love characteristic of God** comes to bear. With the effectuating Elohim-Power in place, it is the grace-giving, agape-loving, covenant-making Yahweh characteristic in and through which God relates to us **personally**. That He chose to create each one of us **personally** is of tremendous biopsychospiritual import. But for His Love directing Power, there would not be the privilege of any kind of blessing afforded us in the *here* or *hereafter*.

Think with me now about how that which is connoted by these two distinct names of God—Elohim-Power and Yahweh-Love—function inseparably in unified fashion in His relationship toward us, and in our "power of our choices" relationship with Him. God has no choice in His relationship with us as He is unchanging and unchangeable Life, Love, Righteousness, Truth, Justice, Grace, Mercy, and Forgiveness. He **is** the Savior. He has no choice but to be What and Who He is, relating to us through these elements of Himself that He **is.** We, however, have the power of our choices as a gracious gift from God. We can choose "yes" or "no" in how we relate to Him.

To be accurate, then, how does Yahweh-God-Love coexist with Elohim-God-Power rationally since EGP connotes power in the sense of judgment and severity? These facets of power will and **must be absolutely** just and severe for anyone outside God's will with no redeeming factor, except that acceptably provided by Himself in the Son. Without redemption, the severity of God's Elohim-Power Judgment is literally **unimaginable in its purity**. In the same way as we cannot conceive what **the purity of the terribleness of Hell** is like, neither can we imagine what the purity of the love of Heaven is like!

Grundmann again closes the gap saying, "His power is not caprice; it is the expression of His will and is thus determined by the content of His will, **which consists in *righteousness.*** The power of God constitutes the inner energy of holiness and gives it the character of [His glory]. The power constituted of holiness and righteousness is effective as **the power of judgment *and* grace**"[56] (emphases added).

The Elohim-Power element of God's character is inseparably constituted with the Yahweh-Love aspects of God's holiness and righteousness nature, **the operation of which effectuates as one and the same** both His judgment **and** grace!

God's wrath is, in this sense, no different than His love. If I'm in His will, there will be "the peace that passeth all understanding" (Philippians 4:7), even in terrible circumstances. However, if I choose to be outside His will, I will automatically be in His wrath not because He is against me, but because, inherent in His holiness, there is a necessary consequence to un-holiness. If **my** choice is to un-holiness, it is not God but I who did it to myself, just like Eve and Adam did. Remember, God **told them** beforehand **what to do, by telling them what not to do to avoid the consequent fearful vulnerability and bondage to *Death*** (as He has done regarding many "controversial socio-politico-religio-cultural issues today (Hebrews 2:15))! God hates sin but not the sinner. Jeremiah 29:11 states, "For I know the plans that I have for you, declares the LORD, plans for welfare and not for calamity to give you a future and a hope" (NAS).

---

[56] Op. Cit., Grundmann, 293.

God is **All-Powerful** and human beings are powerless. As we come to more nearly grasp the Reality of this Truth declared by the Lord, Yahweh, it should instill ineffable gratitude toward Him. **Understanding and accepting that the "Elohim-ness" of God is in the service of His "Yahweh-ness" gives man a sense of relief, hope, and freedom.** Paul describes it to Timothy in 2 Timothy 1:7, "For God hath not given us the spirit of fear; but of *power,* and of *love,* and of [therefore] **a *sound mind*** (KJV emphasis added).

The loving, caring, prayer-hearing, forgiving, covenant-making, and personally relating Yahweh calls forth Elohim-Power to effectuating the overcoming of the world, sin, and death in the resurrection and ascension of His Son, our Savior. Yahweh has directed Elohim, as it were, to serve His Love and Righteousness, as well as His Judgment, to our welfare. **Adopting a submissive attitude before Him, therein being em<u>powered</u> by Him through His Grace, <u>results</u> in <u>recognizing</u>, <u>acknowledging</u>, and <u>accepting</u> the Reality of <u>"What" and "Who"</u> God <u>IS</u>!**

The thusly intellectual, cognitive, and, therefore, willful, God-empowered, biopsychospiritually chosen attitudinal beliefs lead to behaviors which <u>**evidentially**</u> declare the **acceptance** of the above-described "What" and "Who" of God. The acceptance of the Truth and Reality of such unseen, un-weighed or un-measured biopsychospiritual dynamics demonstrates itself in observable and, to some extent, measurable physical activity manifested through a sound mind: producing a sense of present and ultimate Security, even in the face of ever-present and imminent death. It stimulates an attitude of, "Oh Death, where art thou sting?" (1 Corinthians 15:55).

God's Design for "Theory of Personality" – A Paradigm Shift

Creation Power and Resurrection Power each then is this Elohim God Power, as are miracles. This is what any Christian mental health practice is all about and has to offer —- Elohim God Power directed by Yahweh God Love in grace! Any mental health worker, regardless the level, who desires his work truly to be biblically Christian will find here, I believe, a paradigm within which to work confidently before the Lord, the impetus of which is funded by EGP.

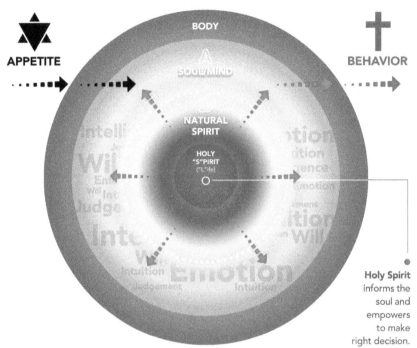

APPETITE

BEHAVIOR

Holy Spirit
informs the
soul and
empowers
to make
right decision.

Remember that **A & B** (the Soul & Spirit) are both of the image of God and are immaterial and **eternal**: (Cf. Pgs 12, 37-38, 53-54, et seq.)

The red represents the Holy Spirit residing and operating in the natural spirit. Regeneration is a spiritual occurance but the event takes place in the spirit. The Holy Spirit is not in the body nor in the soul/mind. He resides in our spirit.

1ˢᵗ & 2ⁿᵈ DEATHS

SECURITY (Heb 2:15)

And deliver them who through fear of death were all their lifetime subject to bondage.

FATAL FLAW ... POWER ... POWER ... POWER

HEB 1:3

The Son is the radiance of God's glory and the exact representation of His being, sustaining all things by His powerful word. After He had provided purification for sins, He sat down at the right hand of the Majesty in heaven.

MATT 4:24

News about Him spread all over Syria, and people brought to Him all who were ill with various diseases, those suffering severe pain, the demon-possessed, those having seizures, and the paralyzed; and He healed them.

EZEKIEL 36:27

I will put My Spirit within you and cause you to walk in My statutes, and you will keep My judgments and do them.

Results of
CONVERSION

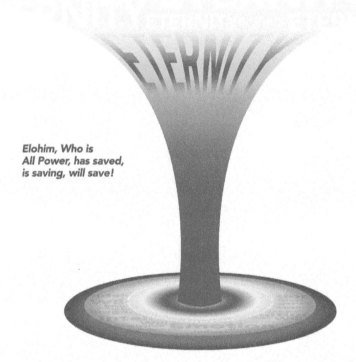

Infinity = Eternal Life

*Elohim, Who is
All Power, has saved,
is saving, will save!*

Without the Elohim-Power characteristic of God, the Yahweh-Love characteristic could hold no more promise or hope of security than any other god because it could not be effectuated! God says we are in bondage because of fear of death. This is where the Yahweh-love characteristic of God comes to bear: the loving, caring, prayer-hearing, forgiving, covenant-making, and personally-relating Yahweh calls forth Elohim-Power to effectuating the overcoming of the world, sin, and death in the resurrection and ascension of His Son, our Savior. Yahweh has directed Elohim, as it were, to serve His love and righteousness, as well as His Judgement, to our welfare. Adopting a submissive attitude before Him, therein being empowered by Him through His Grace, results in recognizing, acknowledging and accepting the reality of "What" and "Who" God is! ETERNAL LIFE!

An analysis of the biopsychospiritual dynamics observed in the clinical situation and a description of their clinical application of this paradigm must wait for a work presently being prepared. For most who participate, by the Grace of God, this leads to biopsychospiritual understanding, which **when applied**, affords a better understanding of God's design of "theory" of personality and the psychology of conversion, and their significant relevance in fostering healing and managing (not controlling) everyday experience in ways otherwise not available by man's intelligence or his science (See diagrams D7b and D7c, pages 115-116).

We must be willing to recognize principles already accepted by many reasoned, unbiased opinions, i.e., Jastrow and Flew noted above. Further, not only they, but, for example, Heisenberg's Principle of Uncertainty, Godel's Incompleteness Theorem and the implications of the Now Physics, as noted by Kenyon, Larson and Ratzsch and others.

Post Note: To make this point of this EGP concept, I offer the following pragmatic consideration:

A convention only for qualified academic and professional scholars was called for the purpose of discussing God. Having looked at all the tremendous intelligent advances of their scientific technology, they concluded "we just don't need God any longer." Next, the most imminent and highly lauded Nobel Laureate confidently volunteered to tell God this unfortunate for Him conclusion.

Informing God, "We're sorry to have to tell you this, God, but, you know, we just really don't need you anymore because of all our intelligence, and technical scientific discoveries."

God responded, "Okay, but, let's have a little contest before you leave."

The volunteer confidently responded, "Okay, what would you like to do?"

God replied, "Let's make a man."

With just a moment's hesitation, the confident scientist said, "All right..." and reached down to get a handful of earth.

At which point, God said, "Oh, no. Ooooooh, no! I love you, but you go get your <u>own</u> dirt!"

CHAPTER 4

Insights for You to Know and Apply

➤ *The problem inherent in each "I" and to which each "I" contributes is and arises from when what I want and what he or she wants is different. We each want what we want right when we want it and both feel we have a right to it! We are offended if it is not immediately forthcoming.*

➤ *God Is Love and Defines Love; Man Does Not!*

➤ *God Is Power and Defines Power; Man Does Not!*

➤ ***God doesn't have a body!*** *He is Spirit! However, He thinks, feels, and speaks of His soul, also; so He has Personhood (another quality of Himself), some of which He imbued in us when He created us in His image. Being in His image, the* **consciously mindfulness of the spirit** *is the operant expression of that inseparable relationship between the spirit and soul.*

118

➢ *The actuality of the reality of the immaterial spirit/soul world has no such limitation.* *The qualitative characteristic in which God's image consists is us, then, it the immaterial, non-physical aspects of ourselves – our spirit and soul – the life in us, and the mid faculty for cognition, reasoning, and* **choice-making***.*

➢ *The spirit and the soul are not the same.* *They are inseparable, but not the same. Likewise, the body is a separate material mass which was caused to become alive by the imbuement of Spirit (life) into it and, simultaneously, imbued with the capacity to think, sense, emote, judge, and choose (or exercise) will.* **Personhood** *was established. The material mass was now the soma or body, and the components of man's total personality were complete as clearly identified by the Lord in the two Scriptures cited above: his spirit, pneuma; his soul, psuche; and his body, soma as stated in the Greek.*

➢ *If you're wrong in believing there is no God, you wagered for 70-75 years of pleasure against constant, unrelenting non-pleasure, against an unimaginable* **eternity** *of unrelenting suffering and misery,* **and are lost** *with no hope of relief! So, then, we are to understand that the brain is not the mind, but the mind is* **a** *function* **of** *the brain as a physical organ. To grasp the full significance of this, however, we must also understand how* **immeasurably different the activity** *of the* **sub***-atomic particles that make up the physical atomic particles that make up the molecular particles that make up the cells, and then tissues, that are then* *organized into what we call organs which then cooperatively interact with one another in a purely physical system we call the body, the soma. So, then, the brain is not the mind nor is the mind the brain.* **The mind, however is a function OF the brain. But only as long as whatever the "I" of "me" is** *(whatever that is),* **is in the body!**

➤ *Being separated from the EGP of God's Holy Spirit and not having the saving redemptive* **relationship** *provided in that Yahweh-Elohim All Loving Power which* **is** *God, man is left with just his natural material body, and only his natural materialistic frame of reference to inform his natural soul or mind!* **the spirit informs the soul.** *It vitalizes our soul/ mind for the expression and manifestation of our invisible individuated personhood* **through** *the body.*

➤ *From before the time we are born, our behavior is influenced by an awareness within ourselves that our biology could stop "ticking" at any moment, and we are* **powerless** *to do anything about it!*

➤ *With the effectuating Elohim-Power in place, it is the grace-giving, agape-loving, covenant-making Yahweh characteristic in and through which God relates to us* **personally.** *That He chose to create each one of us* **personally** *is of tremendous biopsychospiritual import. Without His Love directing Power, there would not be the privilege of any kind of blessing afforded us in the here or hereafter.*

➤ *God is all power and human beings are powerless. As we come to more nearly grasp the Reality of this Truth declared by the Lord, Yahweh, it should instill ineffable gratitude toward Him.* **Understanding and accepting that the "Elohim-ness" of God is in the service of His "Yahweh-ness" gives man a sense of relief, hope, and freedom.**

> ➤ *Creation Power and Resurrection Power each then are this Elohim God Power, as are miracles. This is what any Christian mental health practice is all about and has to offer: Elohim God Power directed by Yahweh God Love in grace!*

CONCLUDING THOUGHTS

One writes a book like this in order to influence the future. I am hoping that this book will stimulate many Christian psychiatrists to practice more fully and effectively. I hope that patients will be better informed so as to choose psychiatrists who can take into account their Christian faith and use it for the greatest possible healing and growth.

A particular motive that I have within the profession of organized psychiatry is to stimulate a demand that Christian psychiatry have its legitimate place as a part of the greater professional institution. We have Chicano psychiatry and Women's psychiatry and Afro-American psychiatry – all the under-represented groups and points-of-view which have special caucuses or professional sections with the American Psychiatric Association. From a psychiatric point-of-view, Christians have been under-represented and under-served.

After the APA stated that "there is no such thing as *Christian* psychiatry," I searched for a method that could be identified as bona fide *Christian*. I have searched for a method of counseling with a body of theory the elaboration of the premises of which were dependent on their derivation from fundamental biblical principles and would support the correlation of certain bone fide psychological principles. A Christian psychiatry doesn't look to be support by any psychological principle. What affords any psychological principle validity is that it corresponds with what God's Word has already told us, not vice versa.

Having searched, I found no such method. However, I discovered that in His Word, God presents His design for "theory" of personality and describes the "psychology of conversion" relevant to the structure of the personality. When understood and is put into practice the psychology of conversion leads, even with the pains of life, to a sense of comfort, peace, and joy by making it possible to essentially eliminate the psycho-spiritually debilitating effect of the fear of death (Hebrews 2:15). The Psychology of Conversion is presented here as a new paradigm for understanding the human condition through the expression of the psychology of everyday living as manifested in inter and intrapersonal relationships intrapersonal relationships (See again diagrams D1, page 4; D2, page 6; D3, page 9; Iceberg, page 11; D4, page 30; D5, page 63; D6, page 98; D7, page 101; D7a, page 102; D7b, page 115; D7c, page 116).

The universality of the questions of life and death, where did we come from, what are we here for, where are we going and what difference does it make (if any) is why there's never been a culture that had no religion. The function of every religion is to address the anxiety (the source of all neurotic symptoms) provoked by the inability of man's intelligence to fathom the reaches of these questions.

The kinship of philosophy and religion also reflects this. Moreover, every experience of anxiety results from being reminded in the situation of powerlessness over mortality. Therein lies an ever-present fear of death. Jesus' incarnation, death and resurrection was to "deliver them (us) who through fear of death were (are) *all their lifetime* subject to bondage." The degree to which comprehending these tenets helps a person adopt a submissive attitude before this Yahweh-Elohim, this "God with all Justice and Loving Power," is the degree to which is provided "not a spirit of fear, but of power, love and *a sound mind!*" This is the "spirit informs the soul...actuality of the reality of the immateriality" work, the very practical psycho-spiritual work, of valid psychology integrated with Christian theology.

Our culture is more greatly challenged with a plethora of societal issues creating much turmoil both within and outside the church. All these decry a strong debilitating secular orientation within the church. It doesn't necessarily mean, however, a lack of interest in spiritual things. To the contrary, surveys have shown significant increases in the number of Americans who say they believe in God. In view of some of the above issues, however, what that means is open to speculation.

As a result of my searching for Christian counseling methods, a significant area of response has been a problematical growth in many methods and forms of counseling deeming themselves to be "Christian." The last century and-a-half has seen the pervasive impact of the religious philosophy of Humanism permeate, not only our culture generally, including the church, but the fields of psychiatry and psychology particularly.

The Humanist Manifesto states that "...we begin with nature not God" and that is their stance today. The put the proverbial "cart before the horse," starting with something which is not really appropriate as far as first things; and, in that, there is a denial of God. So, we must remember the subtlety of the specious plausibility of humanistic psychology's appeal as it was taught to those students and seminarians who unwittingly taught those who then unwittingly teach laymen from the pulpit, in pastoral counseling, and other professional counseling to value as truth the insidious lies hidden in the tenets of Humanism. The Church must recognize that the cultural changes noted above and the turmoil within itself may well be the result of the fact that Humanistic Psychology has influenced the Christian Church much more than the Church has influenced psychology!

Many have been working toward a better balance by attempting to integrate Christian theology with psychology. The need and interest in this are reflected in the fact that various American Christian counselor associations have grown in memberships in a short amount of time. However, my profession's national organization, in its almost militant secular orientation, moved to have it deemed unethical to even present one's self as practicing "Christian" psychiatry "because there is no such thing." And, having practiced psychiatry for more than forty years, I agree with them. That is, there has been no body of hypotheses formulated which assumes a certain set of facts which, when presented with a problem, can be explored, investigated, tested and account empirically for the facts assumed.

Of course, there are differences about theology and methods of worship, which differences define the denominations but do not negate the commonality of being Christian. However, there must necessarily be at least a minimal set of fundamental points of Biblical theology without which no belief system can qualify as Christian. This is what this book is primarily about.

This book, too, relates to and is about Power. It's about all power belonging to God. God is the Source of Power. God is Power. God is Power with loving justice and mercy in all the He is or is known to be or act. Thus, the term EGP as noted earlier – Elohim God Power.

This book is not about influence. And, we're not talking about energy or the expression of energy. Interpreting energy to be the same as power is a big error. Contemporary astrophysicists have said stated that "the universe is God. The laws of the universe...of physics and energy is God." Well, energy, of course, can't be God. God created energy before it was. It's not material in any kind of way. God's Spirit is the Source of Life in us and the Source of all POWER. God created energy as the underlying means – at the nano scale — of systems chemistry including all the scientific laws or principles of how it works. He put the scientific systems together. This is the problem materialists have when confronted with beginnings of the things we don't know. They, in fact, cannot explain or demonstrate with accuracy that which they do not accept. The eminent scientist Robert Jastrow said, "We as scientists should not say that God does not exist because we can't prove that. We don't know that for sure. We cannot disprove that He exists nor, of course, can those who believe that God exists either can they demonstrate it." That's the source of the controversy from a philosophical and religious standpoint over the eons and still is, obviously, if not raging in full dissent one with the other.

There is a fatal flaw both in how we view power during this temporal life and eternity. Moreover, it relates to our saving relationship with God in Christ. Without a source for power there is none. Without a source for life there is none. Today's technology gurus have made the point, "While we've figured out how to transmit data at acceptably high speeds over the air via radio waves, power is a whole different story...What's the #1 deadly flaw of every single Apple, Samsung, and Google product on the planet? ...You still have to plug everything into a power outlet at some point, or else it's dead as a doorknob... And that's true for even your most efficient networked devices..." Every network device on the planet, including the body or the brain – all which are examples of the current hype of "systems chemistry"[57] — has this same fatal flaw. So, these scientific systems relate here with regard to the fatal flaw. Also, it raises both those questions of "What is life?" and "What is death?" The latter question is not normally a point of consideration but is the one that is most critical to human beings or to life and, particularly, to human life.

---

[57] Systems Chemistry w/Teleonomy & Teleology: Recent scientists who have profound academic and public influence, chemist Addy Pross and physicist Peter Hoffman, wrote of their respective thoughts about what life is and as relates to what is termed Systems Chemistry. Each scientist ends up coming from a materialistic frame of reference and Dross believes he explains how chemistry becomes biology at a deeper level of the Darwinian evolutionary process. The conclusion drawn is about "cooperation" and not a reaction when, for example, an atom of sodium is close to an atom of chlorine. They theorize using the biologic terms teleonomy and teleology that there is a sense of awareness or purpose within the atoms when they "cooperate." This is an attempt to simply address some observations. Teleonomy: the quality of apparent purposefulness and goal-directedness of structures and functions in living organisms brought about by the exercise, augmentation, and, improvement of reasoning. The term derives from two Greek words, τέλος telos ("end, purpose") and νόμος nomos ("law"), and means "end-directed"[1] (literally "purpose-law"). Teleology: The study of the structure and purpose of things.

"Bones cannot be quickened into life by manipulation. Only the touch of God can give them life...clear-cut distinction between influence and power. Influence is made up of many things: intellect, education, money, social position, personality, organization –all of which ought to be used for Christ, Power is God Himself at work *unhindered by our unbelief and other sins.* The word *influence* occurs but once in the Bible, and that in Job ... word *power* holds the secret, and *the power from on high...*God the holy Spirit *...giving it a birth from above...*did in a minute what my best efforts could not do."[58]

So, the brain is not the mind: the brain is material and the mind is immaterial. The life is immaterial and without life in the complex systems of the body (the device) —- and there are many who want to approach the brain or body as a computer, or the ribosome within the cell's nucleus as a computer —- then all the scientific laws that regulate and apply to operating those systems are not physical and every one of them has to, at some point, be plugged into a source of power or, they are "dead as a doorknob." It is important to understand the difference between saying that the brain is the same as the mind versus the mind being a function of the brain. The corollary is the equivalent to when the body is *in* the coffin versus standing *by* the coffin when, at this point, the body is no different than the coffin, or even a rock, itself (the atoms being the same identical atoms and being "dead as a doorknob"). If we, including our strict scientists and humanists, can

---

[58] Dr. A. C. Dixon, pg 169 (Springs in the Valley, Mrs. Charles E. Cowman, The Zondervan Corporation, Copyright 1939, 1968, This edition published in 1997)

learn more of what death or the state or status of death is, we will probably invariably arrive at a better awareness or better understanding of what life is! The lingering and confounding question is of the difference between the systems of the body —- likened to a device in systems chemistry —- <u>in</u> the coffin versus the state or status <u>before</u> it was in the coffin. It is a remarkable difference between the substance of the person, with personhood, prevailing before the spirit left the soul and body. That difference is what has been presented in the entirety of this book, in varying degrees and means, using various examples to speak to the same experiential phenomenon: eternal life and eternal death! Remember Galileo remarked, "The Bible shows the way to go to heaven, not the way the heavens go."

There is a <u>specific</u> difference in the religion of Christianity which demonstrated – not just claimed – that there is life after, or beyond, death of the body. It is the only religion in all of recorded history that even claimed that their God died within the physical form and came back to life and was as physical to other humans' senses as He was before He died which is remarkable (to say the least)! Not only was He alive again, resurrected from the dead, and recognizable with all the elements or criteria of determining by biology that something <u>be</u> alive but, beyond that, He was "more than" and exemplified "something more" which transcends the limitations of scientific law. He was no longer subject to the laws of nature because He <u>ascended</u>...which is contrary to everything that we can think of from a material or scientific or physics standpoint.

The promise and hope of Christianity are that through regeneration, you're "plugged in," even after material, bodily death. Through the Power of Jesus Christ Who overcame death, for us, we can rely on the power of being _moving_ from being dead to _moving_ to being as alive again as life can be given the availability of such help to overcome difficulties. Hebrews 2:14-15 reveals, "Since the children have flesh and blood, He too shared in their humanity so that by His death He might break the power of him who holds the power of death – that is the devil – and free those who all their lives were held in slavery by their fear of death. (NIV)" Jesus did this through His sinless life, having performed perfection in the material form and the immaterial kept it righteous, holy and perfect in the material He created.

We necessarily have a conclusion or conclusions to arrive at. Science, to this date, has not given us an intellectually satisfying conclusion because it cannot disprove the actuality of the reality of immateriality nor can religious endeavors leave us with anything more "concrete" than faith. So, we are left with irreconcilable differences between the two which, in and of itself, does not remove the responsibility of the chosen conclusion at which one arrives at and by which lives their life. However, considering both Camus' and other renowned substantive statements that the substantive material realm has no promise, hope or peace because "...the only issue is shall I commit suicide today [with whatever consequence that carries, of which we're not certain other than according to what Scripture says: "...thou shall not murder" '... and if I commit suicide, I have murdered myself..."] and a consideration on a non-substantive basis for reality – between the two realms of consideration – Christianity and its faith walk seems to offer hope and has more peace, comfort and joy.

As one struggles for security fulfillment in this patently insecure environment we call life, it is obvious from historical reality or any objective appraisal of reality to find, observe, grasp, or to know through Christian faith that you have eternal security. Nothing in history provides us that outside of Christianity. C. S. Lewis so poignantly remarked, "I believe in Christianity as I believe that the sun has risen. Not only because I see it, but because by it I see everything else."

One of the purposes of this book is to teach the theoretical construct to others called to do what, at least from my frame of reference and experience by the grace of God, can truly be said to be Christian counseling. It requires one's own personal relationship with God in Christ, Who provides the presence of the Holy Spirit empowering changes of heart, attitudes and behaviors by *choice*; a willingness to continue to "Study to rightly divide the word of truth;" a diligence toward continuing in-depth growth of professional understanding; and a commitment to "love thy neighbor as thyself."

As a psychiatrist I treat both organic and neurotic psychological illnesses. Therefore, in the presentation of clinical studies, I address differences in treatment approaches.

Lastly, inherent is a Christian apology. The proof is in the pudding. Paraphrasing John 14:21, "Love Me; open your life to My love; be obedient; my Father's loving EGP will flow; experiencing Our love; I will become _real_ to you." Hopefully, each reader will ask wondrously with praise, "What am I, O Lord, that Thou art mindful of *me*?"

To conclude, remember the joke when the scientist challenged God:

> God was sitting in heaven one day when a scientist said to Him, "God, we don't need you anymore. Science has finally figured out a way to create life out of nothing – in other words, we can now do what you did in the beginning."
>
> "Oh, is that so? Explain..." replies God. "Well," says the scientist, "we can take dirt and form it into the likeness of you and breathe life into it, thus creating man."
>
> "Well, that's very interesting... show Me."
>
> So the scientist bends down to the earth and starts to mold the soil into the shape of a man. "No, no, no..." interrupts God, "Get your own dirt."

It remains poignant not only for the purposes of this book, and for the lives of its readers, but, too, in light of the words of 1 Corinthians 15:19, "If only for this life we have hope in Christ, we are to be pitied more than all men. But Christ indeed has been raised from the dead."

As ethereal as all this might be, as you might think it to be, please give it some more thought because, as I say, God really ain't stupid and He ain't impractical.

Table of Contents for Case Studies

THE DOCTOR-PATIENT RELATIONSHIP

Introduction to Case Studies

As we look more closely at specific case studies in the application of *Elohim-God-Power* in therapy, I will remind you of some of the concepts I have shared earlier in this work.

The relationship of a patient with a doctor practicing Christian psychiatry builds upon accepted secular practice and, may necessarily, go far beyond it. The practitioner will convey to the patient usual attitudes of interest, warmth, and understanding. In the initial evaluation period, the doctor will also begin to communicate a sense of humility, kindness, sincerity, and an authenticity grounded in Christian love.

We two, doctor and patient, are persons coming together in the illumination of Scripture and for growth in Christian faith.

Because the suffering patient often presents him/herself as a being whose faith is either weak, in the moment, or obscured by pain, it is especially important that the doctor's faith be such that it radiates, as it were, through his communication and working practice. The creation of this therapeutic atmosphere necessarily starts with an inner, subjective conviction of the doctor, i.e., it starts within him. The radiation is strictly objective. Though this recurrent process is difficult to describe, the therapist is really able to operate most effectively when the patient apprehends the presence of the Holy Spirit and is moved to take account of this, to take it into himself. Permit me further explanation...

Instances of such spiritual communication are frequent in Christian counseling practice, though it would take more than a poet—and that an exceptional one—to capture what is brought with the Holy Spirit's presence. I can only suggest in these cases the play of the divine light through the words exchanged, the non-verbal gestures and attitudes, and the therapeutic results. But, the reader who brings Christian faith to these accounts will feel these merciful influences playing upon both patient and doctor, and probably has felt them already as he or she has read to this point.

More easy to describe is the role of theology, of doctrinal belief in Christian psychiatry. Both doctor and patient bring beliefs into the therapeutic encounter. Unless the doctor is a saint, he cannot be presumed to have a monopoly on theological truth. On the other hand, all things being equal, he is probably in a better state of theological clarity just because he is not undergoing the sort of pain—and usually real pathology—that brought the patient in the first place.

It is my duty, therefore, as a Christian psychiatrist to present for the patient's consideration what the Bible says or what he thinks about such and such.

My job is to clarify and elaborate. I don't force an interpretation of biblical truth, but I do present it—from a specifically Christian and helping professional standpoint. If doctrinal issues come up about which I am not knowledgeable or sufficiently prepared to discuss, I can recommend we study the subject together or that the patient talk to a pastor or find some other means. I frankly confess my ignorance or my inconclusiveness, but I try to keep these instances at a minimum, nonetheless ...not by faking knowledge but preparing myself in an ongoing way for such issues. I use biblical study, theological study, training, reflection, meditation on God's truths in Scripture, discussion with experts and those special people who seem to carry the written and living Word within them.

In all such preparation, I try to be a self-aware Christian, in obedience to God's command and call, understanding what I believe and why I believe it, what I don't believe and why. Otherwise, I cannot meet the Christian patient who has doubts and concerns with the offer of some leadership. I don't try and determine what she will believe, not at all. I do bring leadership, however, offering something new, perhaps, that I know is at the very least genuine and, at its highest, is revelation from God's Holy Spirit.

So, it is a delicate process, woven between the poles of humility on the one hand and responsibility for making a helping effort on the other. And this is true, or it should be, of all helping professional practice. I need to study and understand this "Psychology of Religion" paradigm — to do what needs to be done and, moreover, know how it works pragmatically in life.

The Interfacing of Theory and Practice

Theory is important to the practice of Christian psychiatry as it is in any other school or approach. Without theory, we cannot even know if we are doing Christian psychiatry or not. Nor can we build and develop it as a common endeavor. Nevertheless, the essence of our approach is in its practice. No abstract account, no intellectual description, however important these are, can do justice to the essence which ultimately can only be glimpsed in the acting out of the approach, in our penetrating to the essentials of Christian psychiatry as revealed through the study of many practical examples, particular cases.

To do justice to both theory and practice, I will alternate them throughout this discussion, expecting that the approach in both its totality and its essence will gradually reveal itself to the mind, intuition, and heart—to the very spirit of readers. "But the natural man receiveth not the things of the Spirit of God: for they are foolishness unto him: neither can he know them, because they are spiritually discerned" (1 Corinthians 2:14 KJV).

The Influence of Culture on the Counseling Process

The Christian patient who comes to the Christian psychiatrist for help is seldom immune from the deleterious effects of our secular, atheistic culture. He or she brings the whole burden of a brain-washing—a contamination, really, of harmful and incorrect ideas and practices about such subjects as abortion, homosexuality, liberal or social theology, "humanism" and "humanistic psychology" (so-called), violence and criminality, public health and Christianity, teenage pregnancy, the welfare system, bioethics, euthanasia, the genome project, the "right to suicide," genetic engineering, "women's rights," "men's rights," "animal rights," and so forth.

This is not the place to correct, from a biblically-based Christian standpoint, all these perspectives and movements—not to speak of many others. That would entail a major volume, many volumes, of social criticism. Rather, I want to suggest some principles of practice that can help the Christian patients, inevitably affected to a greater or lesser extent by our atheistic culture, who come to us with one or another complaint.

Sometimes, the complaint—say, *depression*—will be seen over time to find its very origin in these secular ideas and movements. In other cases, the process is more difficult. Very frequently, the whole miasma of secular culture must be dispelled by tackling a number of issues that arise, elements of a pattern of conformity to the large society's values that are serving to push the patient away from living his or her Christianity.

Another frequent pattern that must be undone is the dependency fostered by the secular worldview. This can present itself in a patient who has gotten sucked into living his life on welfare, for instance.

Yet another frequent influence of secular society and its thinking that contributes to pathology and/or a patient's letting go of the anchor of his Christian principles is the wildly exaggerated notion of "rights." This undermines personal Christian discipline, indeed, any discipline at all—and discipline is necessary to mentally healthy living. Some patients believe they have many more "rights" than they do. Others are so intimidated by the supposed "rights" of others that they fail to stand up for Christian beliefs and, so, stray from them, or experience painful and unnecessary doubts, confusions, anxiety, and even depression.

The movement for women's rights, while having done important good work, has also tended to poison the relations between the genders. This is a problem that the Christian psychiatrist meets over and over in the forms of marital disharmony, abortion, child neglect, and even homosexuality.

Behind, underlying, all the cases in this book and underlying all theoretical ideas about relationships in Christian psychiatry, is the practical notion of the psychology of conversion. The Christian psychiatrist, ultimately, is in the business of helping the Christian patient to establish a conscious pattern of turning in faith to God and then doing that faith in the world. When treatment reaches the point where symptoms are sufficiently relieved that the patient can be reminded of his faith and get help in clarifying how that faith applies to his lived life, the practitioner has moved the treatment deeper, from the outer layer of the personality—body and mind—down to the spirit and, in particular, to the part of ourselves that has been touched by faith and inhabited by the Holy Spirit. (Faith is an act of man's will but made possible by the Grace of God.) The doctor then assists the patient to develop conscious and active habits of reaching upward, calling on the Holy Spirit to empower his acting and behaving through his own living situation. One's life is his strongest witness.

Thus does the practice of applied faith multiply itself within the patient's spirit or, if you wish, gradually expand. It will never fill the spirit of the patient or of any human being entirely because of our Sin Nature. So, there is a continuing struggle. But, over time, enormous progress can be made in helping patients to lead truly Christian lives. This is not seminary, I insist, again, but Christian psychiatry. There may come a time when a patient wants to go to seminary or there may also come a time when a seminary student drops out of seminary because of what he has learned about himself in relation to his faith during a course of Christian psychiatry.

Christian psychiatrists are healers, not primarily theologians, though they need to use theology, in many cases, in order to promote the spiritual growth of the people who come to them for healing of their pain and suffering.

"ANGIE"

Addressing Medicines, Truth/Reality, Panic Disorder, Depression, Schizophrenia, Bipolar Disorder

I n any approach of psychiatry, the theme of relationship is present in many contexts. In essence, the Christian psychiatrist is generally non-exclusive; that is, he is not afraid to relate actively and deeply to all the realities that are presented to him. And, by the same token, he is never swallowed up by relationships. He always maintains the ability to choose them or to refuse them; he is able to tailor or limit them according to the requirements of faith as they apply to the needs of the patient.

Medicine and Psychiatry

I am often asked if there is a place for medicine in Christian psychiatry. As with many of the insights and practices of secular psychiatry which I have already touched upon, the answer is a definite "yes."

Paradoxically, this relationship can be curiously important for many people. There are many patients, both Christian and not, who don't want to take medicine. Often, these people believe that the spirit, either in them or beyond them, or both, should be enough in all cases to cure them. This latter group is sometimes obsessed by a sense of sin or, worse—and often the same—by a belief in their magical powers, potential or actual, to control everything. And many other people, both Christian and not, are frightened off by reading about **potential** side effects of medicine, especially the patient who, obviously, can be a casual student of the PDR (*Physician's Desk Reference*). For, medicines can be potent and can sometimes even kill you. In fact, if anyone reads the PDR, they'd never take medicines. They will kill you! According to all the stuff they put in there, that something can do such-and-such is not the something as it will or does each time it's taken. If that were so, nobody could take anything and we'd be back like before penicillin and/or thoragise, etc. Thank God for letting us learn about medicine. Other people are afraid to take medicines because they will lose control, or they fear it will make them into someone else—that they will lose their identity, for example.

But Christian psychiatry has a friendly, if somewhat limited, relationship to the use of medicine. And, so, I explain to all these people that there is an element of our mental functioning which is psychological and another which is biological. This one has to do with the brain (as distinct from mind). The mind, however, is a function of the brain: as long as we are in the body, our mind is rooted in our brain. Once again, I clarify for the patient the physical and non-physical aspect of the human being: "Hand me a pound of mind," I ask. They can't.

"Hand me a pound of brain." They don't want to do it, of course, but they know they could. I make clear that Christian psychiatry is inherently related to the non-physical aspect of the human being.

In general, secular psychiatry attempts to reduce or even equate mind to brain. Even Freud, with his neurologist education, hoped this agenda could be scientifically realized in time. Couched in a Christian worldview that the great "I am" created the universe and all that's in it, Christian psychiatry doesn't subscribe to that. It does recognize that while the etiology of every neurotic symptom is a most direct expression of the Sin Nature, organically based psychiatric problems are different. The brain is, after all, physical and it is electro-chemical in its activity. It's made up of electrons, atoms, molecules, and so on. On the other hand, if my brain is outside my skull, there is no mind operating because **I** am not there.

I discuss these subjects with a patient and present for consideration these notions about the use of medicine versus psychotherapy. Some clinicians and/or hospitals in advertisement of their services, as well as TV programs and even newsprint articles, many times state unequivocally that depression, especially, but other conditions as well, are caused by a chemical imbalance. I might then say, "You've probably heard that all depression is due to a chemical imbalance which many times can be found. The question is which comes first? Not only does the brain affect the mind, the mind can and does affect the brain" (*Archives of General Psychiatry*, Jeff Schwartz, March or April 1996). Practically speaking, it is usually a matter of time of some and some (of each). For, when there is some chemical imbalance underlying the problem, we must also inquire to what extent are there psychological factors, also.

I clarify this dilemma by explaining that a certain number of depressed people get better without medicine or psychotherapy. A certain number get better using medicine only. And, a certain number are treated with psychotherapy only and get better. Without question, however, a greater number do get better with a combination of medicine and psychotherapy. Those statistics are well established and contradict the notion that the mind is simply the outcome of brain physiology in the same sense that digestion is the outcome of the stomach's functioning. What shall we do with the ideas about will and intentional action? Such a notion leaves us as mechanistic automatons.

This is a portion of behavioristic and secular humanistic thought and teaching. It is the only conclusion a secular worldview can allow. Secular psychiatry must and does deny anything spiritual. If you can't weigh or measure it, it doesn't exist! Thank God for the hope that's in Christ Jesus, for the God Who affords me my humanity with all that that means!

Panic disorders are also often thought of as chemical disorders in secular psychiatry. So are obsessive-compulsive disorders. In both of these conditions, however, we know that they can be effectively treated with just psychological means (desensitization, for instance)—that is just with the activity of the mind in the course of behavioral treatment.

As an example, someone who fears crossing a bridge can be treated this way and the technique has been done repeatedly. First, the psychiatrist gets the patient to merely visualize the bridge, then visualize coming up to it, then crossing it—all done very gradually. Then, they go out and just look at it, with the therapist perhaps holding their hand or letting the patient hold the therapist's handkerchief or some such variation of support and, finally, crossing the actual bridge through this process of gradual desensitization.

In such instances, no external chemicals (medications) have been placed in the body to impact the biochemistry of the brain. In fact, medicines are used more often than not in such cases. However, the point is that with the appropriate influence of ideas, words, and suggestions, the mind can and does affect the brain, not just that the brain affects the mind. The brain is not the mind. The mind, being non-material like the spirit, transcends the physicality of the brain (which is like the liver or a food or foot or any other body part). (This differentiation will be more nearly appreciated as we come to realize its relevance tied to an understanding of the significance of the bodily resurrection of Jesus.)

So much depends, then, on the individual circumstances of the individual patient. Medication is the most effective means of treating obsessive-compulsive disorder. Imipramine, Prozac, Serzone, Zoloft, and others are very effective. **I use these and**

would never deny or negate medicine, as it is a gift of God. God is not stupid or impractical, as I never tire of pointing out, and we must try not to be so ourselves. There is nothing in the Bible that says we must insult our intelligence to be Christians! Use medicine when it is needed!

These few last years, I have been working closely with a psychiatric nursing home where we have dozens of patients with dual diagnoses—drug addiction and schizophrenia, for instance, or major depression and schizophrenia, and so on. In the process of working with these complexly afflicted people, I have come to affirm that schizophrenia is a biological problem. So are Bi-Polar and Manic-Depressive Disorder and I use the relevant drugs. I also use them in obsessive-compulsive disorder and in some types of unipolar depression, especially recalcitrant, difficult cases; they need to have the chemical element of the diagnosis/disorder treated.

But rarely is the chemical element **all** of the disorder. The remainder needs psychological attention and, for Christians and any man—Christian patients who can use it—biblical principles correlated with the valid psychological principles must be used.

The dream of the purely biological understanding of man, the dream of secular humanistic psychiatry, is a delusion: it is based on a reductionistic, purely materialistic worldview. The Christian's worldview begins with, is an expression of, and ends with, the spirit world. The well-rounded and balanced Christian realizes that the world, however, is hardly **only** spirit, nor is man.

The case of a woman patient I will call "Angie" exemplifies the interplay of medicine in Christian psychiatry.

The Case of Angie

Angie was in her forties when she came, a professor and community activist with two boys and a successful stockbroker husband. They had been married for over fifteen years. She had a family history of depression and also had some relatives with Bi-Polar Disorder. Both husband and wife were self-described "Christians" and she was also a feminist: a very assertive, even aggressive person, a go-getter, and very bright. Like many manic-depressives, she had that likable glow and dynamism in her hypo-manic or manic phases that moves many people to like and enjoy being around them. I particularly respect her commitment to excellence, sharp as could be, and always challenging to me as a therapist to keep ahead of her. I also respected her commitment to the Lord even in her feminism.

She came in first during a depressive phase, but from family history and her own, I soon made a diagnosis of Bi-Polar Disorder which, with time, was confirmed.

I gave her a tri-cyclic anti-depressant, all we had at that time, but I asked her to come for therapy, also, because I discovered that some of her illness was characterological, part of her personality structure. For instance, she was having trouble in school with a male professor who had somewhat more seniority than she had. We have the old authority and, therefore, the control problem again. Every time you have an authority problem there is the control issue. The issue was her promotion. There was a lot of confrontation, then came depression.

This was a complex case, most of them are. I had to ask myself if her depression was just the down cycle of bipolar patterns. I learned she also had an authority/control issue with her husband which also affected her depression. I didn't know what all the strands were yet. People are complicated and Christian psychiatry must use the valid psychological principles just as does secular psychiatry to be alert to every aspect of the human being. It is worthy of note that Christian psychiatry finds the validity of any psychological principle confirmed by the Scriptures and affirmed in their success with practical application to life.

So, we began the psychoanalytically-oriented psychother-apeutic treatment process of exploring her psychosocial and childhood developmental history, in addition to using several medications. This progressed while I continued to evaluate the interactional relationship of her spirit, "soul" (or mind), and body as an adult in relation to her past while the larger picture evolved toward the present.

As time went on, I became more certain that bipolar dis-ease was part of her problem though there had been no defin-itive manic episodes to date. Almost inevitably, however, there were two closely occurring confirming instances. For example, she spent excessive amounts of money on frivolous things—four hundred dollars on various pairs of gloves including silk ones. The other was spending about $25,000 to help a young male poet she had taken on as a protégé. About two months into treatment, her depression began to lift somewhat, and I suggested beginning the use of Lithium for maintenance and the discontinuance of the antidepressant. She liked the way she'd begun to feel, however, and became increasingly reluctant to come in. As a result, she called and canceled appointments and gradually withdrew from treatment altogether.

Then, a few months after our first visit, she calls, makes an appointment and comes in flying: everything is great, she says. Her dress is flamboyant, her makeup exaggerated, her energy fairly bubbling—everything had become excessive.

She made a megalomanic statement: "I'm going to fix that guy at the school. I'm going to change the whole damn system." She prowled the house at night, called people any time of night; she drove fast, got speeding tickets, was often somewhat confused, and exhibited "pressured speech." In psychiatric jargon that is a term meaning compelled and excessively energetic speaking. She was again all caught up in helping this poet, addressing the "whole world" to arrange readings, pushing everyone to acknowledge him as a "genius," all this without sexual involvement, incidentally.

She, her husband, and I sat down to discuss the situation. She was able to see and agreed that some of her behavior was destructive to the family: her suddenly ducking out of the house after dinner, abandoning everyone—which she had never done before—to go to the library to research poetry and, then, not coming home until two in the morning—effectively deserting her family. She might drive to the next city at these times, with the car's motion, any movement, serving to accompany her racing thoughts. Reluctantly but voluntarily, she agreed to be hospitalized. She knew something was not right.

There is a dictum in psychiatry, never try to do psychotherapy with someone who is manic. Therefore, once she got to the hospital, I gave her Lithium and other medicine to bring her down. As she began gradually to see that her behavior had strong destructive effects—on her work, her family and her bank account—my first approach was to be only supportive. I wanted to be available in case she had questions or angry resentments, and only then moving toward trying to help her see, and this was a crucial element in the case, that her husband nor I was trying to hurt her by urging hospitalization. We were all on the same side.

This woman has been on Lithium now for fifteen years and I have also had to use antidepressants during her downs. But she has also been in psychotherapy with me, initially very often in the early years and, now, only coming for six-month checkups.

One of the themes of our psychotherapeutic work was trying to deal with the false notion of the "aristocracy" of her family. This was a gifted girl who grew up to become a general mover in her community through her drive to succeed. Her family of origin, however, was not particularly extraordinary and her mother was a depressive who had demanded the little girl take care of her. All the talk about "aristocracy" was only an unconscious defense against the reality, the "limits" one might say, of having an ordinary family with significant flaws. The defensiveness carried over into other aspects of her life so that many people saw her as someone with a chip on her shoulder. All these past issues hindered her work and in the family, of course, and further fed her depressive tendencies. Working with her on this theme was an instance not only of using an individual psychological approach to the person but also of employing a socio-psychological approach.

Like all of us, Angie resisted these psychotherapeutic efforts to get at illusions because these notions of aristocracy defended her against feelings of being inadequate and ineffective. Her mother, it turned out, preferred another sibling always and, no matter how good a girl Angie was and how hard she tried, she could never cure that adult depressive. Of course, her sense of inadequacy fueled her achievement drive, too: *she had to be the best at everything and, often, she was.*

In addition to psychotherapy, family and marital involvement—family therapy, if you like—was the key element in this case. This is another example of inclusiveness, the relational quality of Christian psychiatry. I couldn't have really helped her long-term without her husband's active participation. At my initiation, he came in and I explained that her Bi-Polar Disorder was physical. And I tried to explain it in such a way that the idea really got across. Very often family members of such an afflicted person are naturally inclined to read their behavior as voluntary; that is, something for which the patient is responsible in a very simple sense. "It's like having diabetes," I told him. "She didn't have any choice about getting it. She just has it." That sort of explanation strengthened his understanding her behavior and what needed to be done to help her—and not just chemical treatment, either.

I explained to him that the disease seems to be rooted in faulty neurochemistry involving the brain cells and doesn't often just go away. It can be managed, however, as a rule. The hard part is getting people to keep taking their medicine because they "miss my highs."

Really, the similarity to diabetes is great—it's a condition that requires daily chemical treatment, one that has nothing whatever to do with their intelligence, morality or their character. The only choice involved is how to respond to the reality of having the condition. There is no choice whatsoever about having it. The most important thing for Angie's husband was that he not react as before to her symptoms: that he not react simply and automatically but, rather, always try and see the underlying condition that may be driving her at particular moments and, then, act accordingly. Above all, he had to understand that his reactions can promote a vicious cycle of counter reactions from her and within her.

"Be a measuring stick for her illness," I told him. "Be someone who, reflecting of her changing states, she can come to trust and feel comfortable about. She needs to know you will not try to control her in this role; remember her feminism."

When you ask, "Honey, have you taken your medicine?" you must learn to do it in such a way that she comes to believe, over time, that you are not reacting in any way so as to try and control.

Eventually, you will reach the point where she will say, with confidence, to your friendly objectivity: "Why do you ask?" You can then calmly point out, "It seemed you weren't able to sleep last night." Out of your concern, if you don't just react to her, she will come to see that you are, in fact, only interested in furnishing her with information.

As is usual in such cases, it took some time to teach the family to do this service for the patient and, therefore, for themselves. [It was, however, fairly easy to get this family to come in to learn what they needed to do and for the patient to accept it; frequently, in manic-depressive illnesses, there is much more resistance on both parts.] So, this is family psychiatric education. And, when it is needed, is frequently a part of Christian psychiatry as it is in secular psychiatry.

As Angie stabilized over time, aspects of the illness came up which demanded specifically *Christian* psychotherapy, however. All along, of course, I have been appealing to the health inside this patient but, eventually, she improved to the point where explicitly bringing in Christian principles was appropriate.

Except for her neurotic elements, she was now relatively asymptomatic. Because she knows I am a Christian and we talk about Christian things as we go along, and she has a sense of my Christian commitment and faith, she trusts me both as physician and as Christian. As is my practice, I hadn't preached to her in any way but I would make an observation to her like: "That's sort of like what happened to Joseph in the Scriptures" and, from such acquaintance with my Christianity and her having come to me as a Christian psychiatrist to begin with, the ground was prepared.

The phone rang one night during a period when I had only been seeing her monthly to check her Lithium level. I had noticed, however, that her mood had been slipping, though it had not been anything grave. "Mrs. ___ is here at the emergency room and she wants to be admitted to the psychiatric ward." When I saw her shortly thereafter, I learned that it was obvious she was in a serious manic phase. She had gotten up in the middle of the night, left the house, and gone looking for the poet with whom she had had nothing to do for a whole year. I also observed her confusion, pressured speech and, in the midst of all this, her clarity about helping herself in this state, "I need to be in the hospital," she declared.

Thus, there had been important learning and self-care. Though, this time, she went from being manic and having the answer to everything for everybody to being severely depressed and not caring whether she lived or died. However, she never lost faith. Like Job, she never lost her sense of her relationship with God even though they both challenged God.

When I saw her in the hospital, she would tell me how down she felt, how sad, how nothing mattered. But when I probed for suicidal thoughts or impulses she said, "I'm not really there yet—but I'm not sure if God's around or not. Why does this keep happening?" So, I clarified yet again for her that this was just a chemical imbalance in her brain cells and that, until she accepted that fact, she would have difficulty in dealing with it and in managing it.

A part of managing anything is to understand its nature. I told her she and the family had made a lot of progress and, although the husband had seen the episodes coming, he didn't get through to me in time—evidence, again, that there is always a resistance to the fact of illness, a resistance to the Truth.

And then I reminded her: "Ye shall know the Truth and the Truth shall make you free." "Truth is Reality," I said. In the original Greek in which the New Testament was written, the word *alatheia* not only means "Truth" but "Reality" also! There's an element of ourselves which is against knowing the Truth, but we need to keep strengthening the part that wants the Truth which will lead to freedom—the freedom to help yourself deal with a condition that you are not in control of, but that you **can** manage.

Because Angie came from a place of Christian counseling, I could help her. Nevertheless, she had to be in a depressed phase, with little or no sense of control, *before* she could hear what she needed to hear. This was a woman who hadn't cried in twenty years, and crying is an authentic loosing of the sense of need to control. It is a way, at times, of being truly—that is truthfully—close to oneself. She had a fear of crying for this reason but in the hospital, at the right moment, she began to cry. Since many types of clinical problems include this trouble with crying, when a patient cries, I know this is an indication of internal progress—of growth. As I told her again, "Angie, you are surrendering to the Truth; you are letting go of some of your rigid defenses and it's not frightening at all. You've really begun to accept the Truth. [Angie, in all her ordinariness; with all her warts, hair, and all.

In other words, "calling a spade a spade!"] Remember, God says that accepting reality as it is, the Truth will set me and you and anyone else who will come to it, free! Certainly, He's talking first and foremost about the Gospel truth of salvation in Christ Jesus, but He's also talking about freedom in this physical reality.

It needs to be understood here that NO PILL, NO MEDICINE, IS GOING TO GET THIS FAR. A PILL NEVER MADE A DECISION FOR ANYBODY!

What Angie is doing at this stage is through her conscious will. She is accepting the Truth, and therefore, she is beginning to change. We are saved by the grace of God, as I told her and, "as long as any of us believe we are in control of anything, we cannot make the same decisions we could otherwise: our perspectives will be faulty and that will lead us to stances and attitudes which are not helpful for oneself. It seems simplistic but it really is just so simple. The reason it's not helpful to us is because it doesn't glorify God's name. Each time I glorify God's name versus my own, He gets the glory, but I benefit. That's why it is stupid not to exercise faith in God. The most intelligent thing anyone can do is to believe in Christ, Angie, and you are demonstrating that you do."

Opportunities for these kinds of interventions occur over and over in Christian therapy and have potent, lasting effects because of their Source of Power.

After she got out of the hospital, Angie took this glimpse of the Truth—she had never really accepted her illness previously, her powerlessness. Though her brain had known it, she had never accepted it with her intelligence—a psychological, emotional, and spiritual acceptance. Her gut hadn't taken in the Truth. Gradually, now, she became more generally accepting and more loving and caring in general. She began to relate to her children differently, not as evidence of her excellence and ability to control the world and them, but as distinct little people with free wills of their own. She began to see that their purpose was not to bring home A's as proof of their mother's effectiveness. She was a tremendous influence in their lives, but she had no real power over them, no control. Influence is not the same thing as power as we will discuss more fully later.

So, Angie became warmer with them, more melting, and also with her husband. There was a compassion in her not there before. She realized that he really loved her—he was not just a man trying to get rid of her problem or one who wanted only to be proud of her. She saw his heartfulness for the first time in his questions about whether, say, she had slept last night. Thus, there was a major affective transformation in her, a free giving and receiving of love.

Cognitive change came as well for Angie. She gradually saw her mother and sister as separate people with their own struggles and existences, over which she had no power. She is not responsible for them, she's not responsible for the whole world. Her drive for participation in the world changed from compulsion to contribution, freely elected. She can even forgive her mother, let her hair down, and breathe easier. She sees that her mother also had an illness, about which neither of them could do that much.

So many changes in Angie, these and more. But does she still have manic-depressive illness? *Yes.*

Has she been hospitalized since then? *No.*

Have there been fluctuations of mood? *Yes.*

On Lithium? *Yes.* But she has new tools to work with, especially in her husband and children. She can ask her husband now, with no fear, no reluctance, "Am I being okay? Did what I say seem out of bounds or off the wall?"

She can ask these questions because she's not nearly as afraid anymore. The part of her psyche that emerges in her now, the part that is stronger, is not any physical part of her, it's not her brain, but it's the spiritually-inspired mind: intelligence, judgment, and will with a greater degree of freedom to see the Truth and act appropriately—an element of that part that is non-physical. It is the non-physical part that is transcendent and sets us apart. That part which confirms our humanity.

We must conclude that it is that invisible and non-material part of us which identifies us in the image of God. "That part which by the washing of regeneration, and (the) renewing of the Holy Ghost" in our natural spirit empowers the renewing of our minds so that we are not conformed to this world but transformed from it. This spiritually inspired mental activity of the mind influences (empowers) (transformed) intelligent judgment and (empowers) influences the will to direct the body (*soma*). Praise the Lord!

"BUCK"

Sovereignty, Power, Unconscious/Iceberg, Depression, Panic DisOrder, Magic

Implicit in using many of these principles is the notion of how we are both unconscious as well as conscious in our psychological life. Secular psychiatry uses this insight, of course, trying to unearth what is hidden, going back to childhood, and so forth—getting to the origins and mechanisms of maladaptive defenses of the self against reality. The Christian psychiatrist will also point out the larger context of a particular defense; the larger context, that is, of the unconscious forces which act in us. For example, the man who gets chewed out at the office and comes home and kicks the dog is not just kicking his long-past or even dead father, he's kicking God, too. He's trying to have more power than he can. The person with a panic disorder ultimately fears dying. The unconscious reasons for the panic deriving from childhood can be brought up and illuminated. Then, in addition, the fact of God's power, too: "You won't die until God says you're ready to die." In such ways, the Christian psychiatry enlarges the context of treatment and of fundamental psychological notions like the unconscious.

I wish profoundly I had been practicing Christian psychiatry early in my career. I could have offered my Christian patients so much more. Apropos of people trying to die before God is ready for them, I recall a markedly depressed patient whom I treated and will call "Buck." He did better, but then decided to stop treatment. I was reluctant for Buck because I knew he hadn't dealt with influencing factors in his personality structure behind the depressive symptoms. He needed to understand his relationship with his father much better and that the confrontations with his bosses that were "depressing" him were authority problems dating back to his childhood with his father. He was still acting today as if he were his father's frustrated little boy, a resenter of authority. This made him hyper-sensitive to any suggesting others made for his work (This doesn't always happen in parent-child dynamics as long as there is sufficient approval or approbation in the sense of D. W. Winnicott "Good enough parenting.").[59] Buck wanted to show he knew what he was doing, that he was in control, and others didn't and shouldn't have power over him. Part of the reason I didn't try harder to keep him in treatment was that it would only have played into his anti-authoritarian pathological personality construction. I tried to communicate with him,

---

[59] *Child & Adolescent Psychiatry, A Comprehensive Textbook*, p. 810, Edited by Melvin Lewis, 2nd Ed., 1996

challenge his understanding, but I had to be careful not to stimulate him by over-challenging his sensitivity.

Finally, he decided to leave anyway and six months later, the emergency room called me and said the man had a bullet wound in his head. His lack of understanding of the dynamics of his personality had led him back into depression and he had tried to kill himself: once again, a trying to take God's power. However, God had His own ideas about when this man would die. In the parking lot of the city's largest shopping center, the man shot himself with a revolver. But, Buck didn't die. The bullet entered the brain all right and lodged on the opposite side of his head. The results covered him with spurting blood, but, actually, it didn't even knock him out. So, he picked up the gun, again put it to his temple and pulled the trigger three times. It had jammed. Still determined to die and to take his **own** life, so hungry to believe he was in control, he started the car and drove it as fast as he could into the biggest pole he could find. That didn't work, either. God said, "Nope. Not now!" He could have fallen twenty stories and the outcome would have been the same. The whole upshot of the incident, of this unconscious belief in magic that he could, in fact, decide and determine how and when to die—that he had power—was a slight, chronic arthritic pain in his left tempora-mandibular joint.

About four to five months later, Buck asked to come back to treatment. As he worked out the childhood relationship with his father (having asked eventually to do), he was able to reconcile with his father who, as noted earlier, had been dead for several years. Much of this was resolved through the psychological transference with me which is what I'd tried to help him do before he quit earlier. The intensity of the fear and pain encountered was what he was trying to deny and avoid in the first place. That's why he reacted by both leaving treatment prematurely and by trying to kill himself. What distortion! How unnecessary! The unconscious material was unearthed and the conscious intelligence, judgment, and will, as functions of the ego, could be applied to it to put it all in proper perspective.

How much better we could have worked on Buck's whole unconscious material if he had been a Christian and I had been practicing Christian psychiatry at that time instead of secular psychoanalytic psychotherapy. What a striking example of God's having all power! Man and the Devil have none! Not even with all the technical advancements in medical science could a neurosurgeon have placed the smallest probe through that trajectory path without any residual effect. If so, he would go right through the base of the brain where the regulation of blood pressure, heart rate, respiration, body temperature control, etc., take place. Yet, a piece of lead about the size of the tip of a little finger tore through this area without effect.

Buck solved his problems with authority and recurrent depression, but he didn't acquire that higher quality of life, that higher sense of security that Christian psychiatry can foster by working through an experiential understanding of the diagrammatic representation of the Psychology of Conversion. He won't have the "materials or stuff of faith" to work with when he comes up against other challenges in his life. He will also be much more apt to get depressed again than someone who has really learned about limitedness, faith, God's Power, and that it's okay that we are not in **control** —- of anything, not even of our own life **or** death. This man's "cure," to use an old-fashioned term, is much more restricted than it could have been. We can do so much more fundamental work in helping people in Christian psychiatry.

"HENRIETTA"

Depression, Anxiety, Guilt, Grief, Shame, Anger, Confusion, Death, Power, Psychology of Conversion, Narcissism, Self-Absorption

The case of Henrietta particularly illustrates how rapid spiritual progress can be made in a younger patient who came to treatment because of "tension, restlessness, and depression." From a psychiatric standpoint, depression was her primary symptom. Though anxiety and depression together are not at all unusual, in her case the anxiety was severe enough that I treated her with medication for both depression and anxiety. Though I prescribed two medications in this case to begin with, I knew very well that the medicines would not resolve the conflictual emotional problems that were the underlying cause of her pain. If she was going to change her**self**, she would need more than medication!

In taking her history, I learned many things about her and her family, but I was particularly struck by her almost casual mentioning of an early abortion she had when she was seventeen.

She became pregnant, and though she had misgivings and talked about them with her friends, her parents, and even her minister, she finally decided to have an abortion. She described all these people as very rational, "liberal and reasonable," and because her parents particularly felt it was the most "reasonable" thing, and in view of the fact that her minister did not specifically denounce it as being against God's will as stated by Him in His Word, she decided to go ahead and go through with it.

I took note of this event, though I did not say anything about it at the time. Instead, I waited until the medications had brought her some relief and her ego was less clouded by anxiety and depression. Then I began guiding her back to the abortion incident because I knew by then that she had not dealt with the tremendously significant feelings that she almost certainly had had about it. (It is my opinion that no female can know she is pregnant and not be affected by it at some level within her being since God created her for such as this.[60])

Over a period of three visits, during which the abortion was a focus, a degree of both depression and anxiety returned to her. She had anxious dreams, for instance. She was not in as bad shape as when she had first come in, but some agitation had returned. During the third session in this sequence, she was using the couch and talking about a dream. Gradually, she stopped speaking

---

[60] See my article, *Magnificence of a Woman,* published in the Louisiana Psychiatric Medical Association, p. 23 (Summer 1995), where I state that a woman must employ several, if not many defense mechanisms to isolate herself mentally from the truth of her biology. This alludes to and is akin to the underlying dynamic of a lesbian who wants to be pregnant and/ or wants to have a child.

altogether. I allowed the silence for several minutes. Then I asked her if she could share with me what was going on—I realized this was a resistance and I encouraged her to say whatever was in her mind.

No response.

"What are you feeling, Henrietta?"

She began to sob silently from her abdomen. The more she sobbed, the more the clutching of her breath moved up into her chest.

"Henrietta, see if you can put into words what you are feeling," I encouraged her again very tenderly.

She sat up, covering her face with her hands, and began wailing, truly wailing: "I – I–I killed my **baby**! I killed my **baby**!"

Tears were streaming down her face.

Once her wailing broke the dam of feeling, I only needed to foster a process of inner self-realization that tended to flow of itself. She had realized the magnitude of what had taken place. Her horror and guilt at her role and her anger at her parents, especially her mother for allowing her and even encouraging her to do the abortion, all flowed out. She also realized clearly in recovering these unconscious feelings that God was the source of all life and children are a blessing—she'd had two after marriage. She realized further that her mother's "reasonable" view of abortion might have led to her having been aborted herself by her mother, as some fear of the mother had always been there and it had been heightened after the abortion incident.

The point that must be emphasized, however, is that as she began to work through her real feelings and put them together with her undistorted religious beliefs, she began to be able to more and more **do** faith — "Walk the walk, etc.". That is, to behave the belief! First, she departed from many of the social beliefs of our time which she now was understanding she had so unconsciously fallen into—beliefs about the high place of convenience, of personal and family economic position, of so-called "quality of life" issues, by which is often meant seeing people as consumers and "*self*-realizers."

From the breakthrough of insight into masked and hidden emotions and her seeing their relationship to her Christian faith, she received more faith and more light. She became clearer about the nature of man, about herself in relation to God—God's bounty, His protection, His provision, and His being the Source of all life. Because of Him, she knew and reaffirmed (more points in the inner circle of our personality diagram) the **meaning** of life. The "stuff" of life is not in material "having," but in the spiritual, emotional interchange in relationships. In this case, it is the relationship of a young woman's femaleness with the conceiving of the conception of her unborn child who she is going to "mother." This same element of human nature within a lesbian female accounts for the psycho-biologically determined desire for children. It is inherent in being female.

Thus, what Henrietta began to do was to **exercise** faith, not merely believe and have faith. She began to realize that she had repressed and denied something elementary, basic, and therefore, very meaningful in her life. Encouraged by her parents with their weakened sense of faith, her faith had been weakened. As the pain out of her past came up, she became able to reassert her faith. She asserted it. She told me the "meaning of life is not having comforts, a bigger apartment, and more money to buy more things." She saw clearly that these were just power moves, attempts to pretend that we have power.

I told her at one point: "Hitler wanted power and he had what man would call power for thirteen years. He believed that he was omnipotent because it seemed to him that he could avoid his own death. All that strutting and puffed-upness — at the bottom of all that was his trying to deal with that sense of vulnerability which is a part of each one of us. He was trying for transcendence in all kinds of ways—ritual, idolatry, sexual exploits, and murder. But let me point out the reality, the truth—Hitler is just as dead as all the millions of Jews, Poles, and gypsies he slaughtered. The drive to power is the fear of death. Hebrews 2:15 says, 'And deliver them who through fear of death were all their lifetime subject to bondage' (KJV). Howard Hughes is just as dead as the poorest pauper who never had a dime's worth of economic clout. It is only in accepting the reality of our vulnerability that wisdom can come."

I waited a few moments.

She seemed to waver between thoughtfulness and a subtle radiance: "I agree with you, Dr. Lew. I know that's the truth."

We were getting her into the importance of worldview. In Christian psychiatry, the collision between a Christian worldview and that prevailing in our society is frequent and, necessarily so. The worldview of every society ultimately is necessarily materialistic, at least in action. Materialism relates to determinism to the degree that our actions are determined by our society, biology or whatever. But the meaning of life to a Christian is personal and interpersonal, not materialistic: our vertical relationship with God and our horizontal relationship with others as illuminated by that vertical connection. Without a relationship with a personal God Who has the ability to do something about my condition, life is just a vacuum, an existential vacuum. God's power is evident for us, not only in the miracles in the Bible, but in the miracles which each of us, if we allow ourselves to, can become aware of in the course of our lives.

I can't answer the Psalmist's question: "Oh God, who is man that You would give him consideration?" But by using my intelligence, I can be thankful for this and then begin to do what I call "exercising pieces of faith." We don't ever have perfect or ever-abiding faith: we are only capable of doing "pieces of faith." Our only option is "faithing" intermittently, in between sinning.

It was very easy to explain these ideas to Henrietta because she was, in fact, quite spiritual. Yet, we were talking about her living her faith, really, making something of a U-turn by living her Christianity and putting materialistic values in their place. Thus, it was useful to sketch the dynamics of living faith to her.

"God responds to my little acts of faith. I experience that response. My faith closes the gap with God and He responds to me. This bridge of faith lets me experience God's presence with my very senses: I touch, see, hear, feel, and smell Him. I experience God with my body, my existential self. In this process of repeatedly exercising faith and experiencing God's response in physical reality, I gradually come to a belief in Him. As a human, I don't have the capacity to believe at first. Before belief comes faith which you have, Henrietta, and you have more of it since you broke down and cried and owned your guilt and shame and anger about 'killing your baby,' as you put it. Sometimes, however, it is enough faith to acknowledge our lack of it and ask for help toward it. This is one of the meanings of the Doubting Thomas story. That story is a paradigm of this process of reaching toward God (faith) and experiencing a response. Jesus didn't force Himself on Thomas, He just offered him evidence."

"As you go through this process over and over, exercising 'pieces of faith' and then having God's response," I continued, "your faith will become intelligible and your belief understandable. You will come to know what you believe and why you believe it, and what you don't believe and why. But faith precedes belief or understanding, just as with Peter when he was able to walk on water, but when he tried to understand and took his gaze away from Christ, he just sank."

"This process of conversion is at work in you. I have seen it over and over working with Christians and seen them make profound changes. In your feeling of deep guilt, you saw that even though others had influenced you, there was part of you not able to actually control your behavior at that early time in your life, but still substantial, that had opposed the decision. The unexpressed or, at best, inappropriately expressed and, therefore, unresolved, conflictual emotional energy of that part of you ultimately resulted in your symptoms. True enough, because of your commonality with those who were advising you at that time—more specifically, your sin nature and its worshipping of convenience, you had accepted these other influences. But God was chasing you, the Holy Spirit within you was convicting you and, like Jonah, you couldn't get away."

At this point in therapy, Henrietta really began to realize she was no longer a child, but a separate adult person with the power of her choices and its concomitant reality of personal responsibility.

"You know, I really am angry at my mother. I wonder why she or any mother would go along with that. That's part of what my dream was about—in the dream, I was aborted. It *feels* like by aborting my baby, I aborted part of myself, but I also feel somehow that my mother aborted me in her abortion advice. Part of me wonders if my mother ever really loved and wanted me. I wonder how inconvenient it would have had to have been before she might have aborted me?"

Henrietta quickly moved from lying on the couch to sitting, thinking, and declaring herself this way, all of which derived from that work in the previous session with the sobbing. The relevance of her mother's easy willingness to advise abortion and Henrietta's problems with self-esteem became clear. She also dealt with her doubts and anger toward the church.

"How could they do that? 'I knew you before you were formed in your mother's womb,' the Bible says. How could the church not remember that and have encouraged the abortion?" Finally, her anger at herself emerged, at her being pliant.

She owned, after all the defensive anger at others, her own responsibility, stating, "Before God, I'm the only one responsible."

Without being fully aware of it, she was relating to Psalm 51:3-4, "For I know my transgressions, and my sin is always before me. Against You, You only, have I sinned and done evil in Your sight, so that You are proved right when You speak and justified when You judge [me]" (NIV).

This was one of those cases that just flowed, and in the half dozen sessions, I only needed to foster and clarify a process that moved by itself. Because she had faith and was a Christian she could, in the end, accept God's forgiveness of her guilt. Through ventilating the anger, she no longer condemned herself to depression and anxiety. She could smile and she became more affectionate than she had ever been to her husband and children. She became free to be herself.

Part of that new selfhood was that she no longer had the fear of getting pregnant again, which had been inhibiting her sexual life with her husband. Now, she felt that she could live with whatever God had in mind for her—believing God would provide whatever He saw as necessary.

During the course of this work, she also began to feel freer to go to church more often and without the resistance she had been feeling for years. Then something came up in a sermon about God the Provider which had a big effect. The minister was talking about when Joshua and Caleb were sent to scout out the Promised Land. All the others were afraid to go because they had heard that there were Giants in the land and "we are so few." But Joshua and Caleb said: "God is with us. He will provide." God did provide with water out of the rock, manna, and physical provision—all these powerful symbols came up in the sermon and, of course, life eternal.

The meaning hit her: "I can afford not to worry about tomorrow, being anxious for nothing. I don't have what I need, but I have the Source available to me. I don't have the Holy Spirit's power, but it is available to my life twenty-four hours a day in any and every situation."

Her confidence took a giant leap, almost by itself, without my doing very much. She had grown in the Spirit, receiving much more of God's grace beyond her own salvation, and being able, as an adult, to manifest it in the world. More humble and tolerant, she became a better witness for God because she didn't **need** the approval of others. She came to realize her uniqueness as a human being, nothing special but not another one like her. And, so, she became more effective, loving, and whole and it was a wonderful thing to see. So it is, that psychiatry and spirituality can come together in Christian psychiatry.

Note: It's interesting to note that many lesbian "couples" decide to "become pregnant." It is a woman's femaleness which "understands" and stimulates the "mother" instinctual response which is instantaneous at the moment of quickening. The moment of that first recognizable movement of the *life* in her womb. The life placed there by God and God alone since He is the source of all life, her conceiving of the conception of her unborn child, who she is going to *mother*, is the basis for a lesbian's desire for a child. That God-given psycho-biologically determined intrinsic quintessence of being female—the capability to bear children—is the operating dynamic with these females, also. God purposed this in females as He purposed other inherent characteristics in males. In a brief paper published by the Louisiana Psychiatric Medical Association titled, "O, The Magnificence of a Woman," I attempted to present the essence of God's purpose in creating "male and female created He them" (Genesis 2:27 KJV) by focusing on the *complementarity* of the differences between the sexes. The emotional dynamics of the polemics of the dialectic process which takes place within the differences between females and males certainly recognizes the opposites involved, but we should understand that doesn't mean inherent opposition! It is important to recognize the relational difficulties which seem to arise and abide in the insistence on oppositional polemics and the denial of the intended (by God) complementarity. In the psycho-bio-spiritual qualitative element being referred to above, I tried to grasp and present again here in this quote: "What it is that makes my wife distinctively a woman (including its quintessence—the capability to bear children—given only to the female), and her willingness to express it in relation to me flowers the potential in me to be fully, comfortably, healthfully, and happily a man. There is a magnificence in this. A transcendent magnificence which is intrinsic only in a woman—for a man and, I dare say, vice versa." This is not by accident!

If lesbian homosexual orientation were genetically determined, as purported by some "scientists," then that same genetic biology would seem to be more pervasively effective and exclude the desire for motherhood since homosexuality is utterly contrary to the drive for procreation. It also contradicts that Darwinian icon "natural selection" in that it leads to destruction of the species rather than fostering its progress.

Also, what a trick God has played on those He created with no choice of sexual orientation. Genetic determination describes no choice of color of hair, body structure, color of eyes, etc., because it's "in the genes." If He creates them with no other option but homosexual orientation and then very clearly condemns the very thing He created (which He unquestionably does in His Word, the Bible), then He not only contradicts Himself but goes against all the characteristics of righteousness which He wants us to believe about Him.

"JULIA"

Depression, Guilt, Belief in Magic, Perfectionism, Reality, Habit Pattern of Reaction, Iceberg/Unconscious

The case of a woman I will call Julia illustrates some of the concepts listed in the previous chapter and how some of those as briefly defined there can manifest themselves in the consulting room.

Julia was a heavy-set but neat and attractive woman, well-dressed, grayish blonde, upper-middle class, articulate, and a self-described "Christian." Like so many of my patients, she came to me in part because I am a "Christian psychiatrist." She had been married for twenty years and had two teenage children. She was the sort of outwardly chipper and successful person whose friends "would never dream I was seeing a psychiatrist." Whatever the friends may have thought of her, she revealed herself to me as "very depressed." Moreover, she was "overwhelmed with a sense of guilt" about previous life events and things that had happened before her marriage.

"You've just got to help me not to feel so guilty. I know, as a Christian, that God has forgiven me. I teach it in Sunday School and I believe it, but I just can't forgive myself."

Naturally, my first order of business was to look at the depression and see if it was one that should immediately be treated with medication. It was and an appropriate anti-depressant was prescribed. I began to see her twice-a-week to find out about her family situation and what factors in the past might be contributing to her sadness and guilt. Within a few weeks, her depressive symptoms were somewhat relieved. It evolved that she loved her husband and her family was a "good, solid one." But in the recent months, she had been tormented by guilt memories of adolescent sexual experimentation. It turned out that what she was talking about had been "only petting" with another boy or two before she had met her husband-to-be.

Over and over, however, she insisted, "I know God has forgiven me, but I just can't forgive myself."

As any analytically trained psychiatrist would, I wondered within myself what might have happened recently to have precipitated this relatively sudden eruption of *such* memories with *such* intense feelings of *such* guilt that it "even was too much for God." Among several things that entered my mind was the possibility of the pressures of another man in her life at the present time. At first, however, was not the time for any more direct inquiry or confrontation with such a possibility.

After a few weeks of our work together, when the medication had offered some benefit and she had come to have some basic trust in me and our therapeutic relationship, I came to see that, yes, an attraction to another man had, in fact, probably precipitated her current guilt feelings and depression. There were also other unresolved guilt and anxiety issues involved from her early sexual experience in the teens. She was miserable with guilt, as she said many times and, at a certain moment, after discussing her childhood, parents, and other history from a psychoanalytic perspective we did have positive but limited results.

Given those results, I finally asked her, "Julia, you say you are a Christian: are you willing to discuss these guilt feelings from a Christian perspective now?"

When she said she was, but then repeated over and over that she couldn't forgive herself, even though she knew God had, I said, "It sounds like you're generally interested in pleasing God in your life. But in this instance, it sounds like **you** are being more demanding than God Himself would be. Isn't that a prideful attitude—I'm bigger than Him?"

She recognized my little mimicry of her attitude almost at once. In Christian terms, she saw that she was "putting herself on the Throne." She was doubly flabbergasted because she hadn't been aware of it at all. Then, almost immediately, she felt quite guilty for that—clearly this was her characteristic way of reacting. This is an example of what I mean when I talk about a habit pattern of reaction.

I continued to try and increase her awareness from a Christian perspective of what this habit meant while, at the same time, tracing its roots in the general way of psychoanalysis.

"You can continue to feel as guilty as you seem to feel you need to, or we can take a look at how, right now, you are demonstrating the very habit pattern whose consequent suffering brought you here. You are, this minute, showing both of us the pattern you've been unconscious of—an automatic falling into guilt feelings."

I explained some more of what the unconscious is and how big a part it can play in influencing our thinking, our behavior, and ultimately, our very lives. She told me quite clearly that she wanted to look into this unconscious habit pattern of feeling guilty. We did, though I won't go into those details. We talked about the fact that there is such a thing as realistic, appropriate feelings of guilt and, also, an inappropriate, unrealistic sense of guilt. She had said from the beginning that her guilt feelings about adolescent sexual experimentation were now inappropriate and I agreed with her. Then we went on to shining some more Christian light on her situation. We went over the adolescent adventures, I reminded her several times of her acknowledgment of God's sovereignty, and of the Divine forgiveness for those events that she herself had been certain she would receive even before she came to see me. By such means and others, the habit pattern of guilt feelings was gradually weakened. Finally, after she had come to understand that I could accept her humanness, we could go to the reality of the other man.

"Why have you not told anybody that you're coming here?"

"They'll think I'm not as good as I think I am and they think I am."

"What are your concerns? Do you suppose it really would be unheard of that these friends wouldn't see a man at a red light that they think is attractive? And that they would never wonder what it would be like to be in bed with him? Do you think they would never have such thoughts or feelings?"

"Sure. I guess they could have such ideas."

"Apparently, you feel extremely different then, because you seem to think a real Christian would not have such ideas or feelings or images?"

"Well, I suppose most would (long hesitation). But a saint wouldn't."

"But there are lots of records of saints having such kinds of feelings. Luther even says, 'Sin and sin boldly!' What did he mean? I'll tell you. Luther recognized that he was a sinner. Now I ask you, what kinds of people are there in the church?"

"Well, all kinds, I suppose."

"Right. But when you come right down to it, there is only one kind of person in the church: sinners."

One of the problems Christians bring to psychiatry is an unconscious, conditioned by infantile understanding of the Christian basics. A child might be so overwhelmed by a sense of sin, he might grow up never letting into his consciousness the adult awareness, "the ego awareness" one might say, that all people are sinners.

"By the grace of God, in church," I continue, "there are those who are saved sinners and then there are those who are unsaved sinners, but all are sinners. However, it seems to me that you have some question about **your** own status as a sinner. You think you find yourself with thoughts or feelings that Jesus wouldn't have, nor Mother Teresa, Billy Graham, the Pope, or the Southern Baptist Convention President. Even my Mama was a terrific Christian who was also a sinner and I'm sure, at some points in time, had such thoughts and feelings. (When I bring in my Mama, patients usually feel the force of my own seriousness as I make this point to them, reflecting back to their adult awareness what they already know, of course, but which is clouded by younger feelings buried, until this point, in the unconscious.) The President of the United States and the characters in the Bible are all just people like you and me. Really! David was acknowledged by God as a man after His own heart, but didn't David sin with Bathsheba? He had feelings that were stimulated when he saw her and sent her husband into the front lines knowing full well he would be killed. Then, taking her as his own wife, wasn't that very sinful? How could it be, then, that he was 'a man after God's own heart?'"

At this point, I just wait. I turn the process over to her. In the long silence that follows, she's more or less forced to deal with aspects of her own spirituality as opposed to child-based religiosity. As it turned out, I allowed the hour to end in this silence and I sent her home with the question. In fact, the question goes home with her, whatever I do. It works on her. She is forced to face reality.

Not that the process ends there. I guided Julia over the ground from different perspectives, coming at the same material with various concepts embodied in the key words previously noted.

At another session, I asked at an appropriate moment: "Do you believe in magic? It seems that I am hearing a part of you that seems to believe in magic?"

"What are you talking about, Dr. Lew, part of me that believes in magic? What do you mean?"

As she will eventually grasp, I'm trying to show her that a part of her wants to serve God and does, in fact, do so, and another part wants to sin and operate from her sin nature, and in fact, also does so.

"Let me put it a little differently," I said. "Can you fly?"

Shaking her head, she said, "No."

"But," I said, "There seems to be a part of you that thinks you can be perfect; that you can perform perfection. It would take some kind of magical power to do the impossible, would it not? Yet, that's what I hear a part of you saying to yourself. Do you know anybody who doesn't sin? Doesn't it say in Romans 3:23, 'All have fallen short of the glory of God?' and in 1 John 2:8 that 'If we say that we have no sin, we deceive ourselves, and the truth is not in us?'"

What I am trying to do in such a session is to get the Christian patient to face his/her own spirituality. At this point, she was having an interaction not so much with me, but within herself, before God. She was being forced to come to some kind of clearer and deeper realization about the possibilities of her own perfection and, contrariwise, about the perfection of God.

"Julia, I recall you have accepted Jesus as your Savior, right? Remember Nicodemus, '...Ye must be born again to see the kingdom of God...' and John 14:6 says, 'none come to the Father except by Me?'"

"Yes. Yes."

"But there does seem to be a part of you that seems to believe that you can fly or do the impossible. If you could fly or do the impossible, wouldn't put you on the same level as God? Perfect? He performs perfection and, here, you are doing the same thing. You are asking yourself to take the verse from Matthew, 'Be ye perfect even as I am perfect' in some very impractical and unreasonable way. But God ain't stupid and He ain't impractical. He clearly does not mean for you to **perform** the impossible in this world, for that would be like saying that Jesus, our Savior, didn't need to come and save **you** by dying for you. That you can perform perfection on your own and, therefore, you have no need of Jesus' intervention on your behalf."

At this point, at *such* a point, I was challenging her frame of reference. She was intent, listening with her whole being, and struggling. She even began to cry. She was starting to realize that she's been blaspheming God and challenging Jesus. At this moment, she was nowhere but here, present in the therapeutic encounter. Depending on her affective state, her degree of distress, I may then say something to soften her suffering.

"Listen. I know that with your conscious intelligence you don't believe in magic. With your gumption, I know that you know better than that. I know that with the realistic, healthy, more nearly reality-oriented part of your mental functioning, you know you can't fly. You're not stupid. However, alluding and linking back through the entirety of our discussions to now, it would take some kind of magical power that, realistically, you know you don't have. Certainly, you know consciously that you're not God, and therefore, can't perform perfection. It's the immature, unhealthy, unrealistic part of you. That part is primarily operating under the influence of your sin nature, quite unconsciously, and therefore, at present, outside your awareness and understanding that we are working on. This is what has been giving you the problems. That's what we are trying to deal with here, the part of your sin nature which is causing you problems."

"This narcissistic part of you—let me call it that for now and explain exactly what it means later—believes that you are unlimited, that you can do the impossible and that you are, in fact, equivalent to God. That is exactly what the sin nature is all about. In it, we all do want, in fact, to be God! Each and every one of us does," I said, smiling at her, to reassure her of the normality of all this, the comicality of it, and, even so, the security that every Christian truly has in his or her salvation.

"That's the very reason Jesus came and **performed perfection**," I said very slowly, "for me and for you. He died for us, for me and for you, did what we cannot do, could not **possibly** do for ourselves. In other words, God, Who is holy and perfect, makes no demand in the words 'be ye perfect,' but makes a promise. No human being can be perfect, but God can raise us to perfection at the end of things. It's not perfection but direction."

"Meanwhile, God has come in the form of man, Jesus, to relieve us of Adam's curse. He came in the form of man! At once, one hundred percent human and one hundred percent God. God incarnate! What does that mean that God, Who is non-material, non-physical, came in the flesh, just like me and you, just as much human as me and you? What are your thoughts?"

Here I was silent for a while and then I say, slapping my arm deliberately several times, "It means that He came like us: **limited**. He could bleed, hurt emotionally, and be subject to **temptation** just like me and you. And, I am not talking just about three days up on the mountain. Hebrews 4:15 says, 'we can't have a high priest who does not know of our infirmities but who was tempted just like you and me and yet was without sin' (NAS). Speaking personally, that boggles my mind. I just can't relate to never having sinned. Not even once! Not even a little white lie or something! I just can't comprehend that. All I can do is be grateful. Praise You, Lord, and I am grateful for Him. His sinless perfection as Savior, then, He can go on to say —therefore – 'come boldly unto the throne of grace that we may obtain mercy and find grace.' But I **am** grateful for it. And, therefore, He says, 'Come boldly before the glory seat of God to seek succor in time of need.'"

"We can come confidently, not because we are so faithful or good or perfect, but because He is. He has rolled out a red carpet by taking on our human burden while remaining sinless, perfect, God."

Naturally, one does not wash away most of the traces of a pseudo-Christian perfectionism in a couple of sessions. Julia and I kept returning to the problem. It was so deeply ingrained as an emotional habit and pattern of reaction that she had to be taught to learn how to recognize when it presented itself in its various forms of situations. I would expand on the theme of the difference between her (and all the rest of us) and Jesus, our Savior. Again, there is here a theological concept that may seem confusing, controversial, and even perhaps to some at first glance, to be heresy. However, it must be addressed and dealt with because of its biblical common sense. Nothing about it challenges, differs with, or even remotely lessens or demeans anything at Who or What Jesus is or was. It challenges, changes, or refutes nothing about "in the beginning was the Word (the Lord Jesus, the Christ) and the Word was with God, and the Word was God, and the Word became flesh." Like the rest of the Scriptures, God has given them to us for our instruction. It is the "how-to" book. He's given us the Scriptures to instruct us how to **use** and **apply** the principles He's presented there to help us to learn how to **live**. To help us translate the reality of the principles of spiritual truth presented there into the practical application with the experience of this physical material to which we find ourselves exposed. The purpose of applying scriptural spiritual truth is for the exercising of faith and to receive the promises offered in "...[the] Lord Jesus Christ, which is our help!" (1 Timothy 1:1 KJV) and "In Whom are hid all the treasures of wisdom and knowledge...For in Him dwelleth all the fullness of the Godhead bodily..." (Colossians 2:3, 9 KJV).

I will say here that the Bible is the most practical book ever written. I emphasize this again because the concept I'm going to introduce has its significance in understanding how to handle some of our own practical experiences.

What is the theological concept? Ultimately, more than a concept, it is that Jesus could not have become the Christ from a pragmatic standpoint until He died without having sinned. Not until He had **performed** perfection in the flesh, bodily, did He attain the impossible to bring the concept to concrete reality. He was subject to, as stated in Hebrews 4:15-16, all temptation such as you and I. He had to exercise faith, not just for three days up on the mount, but for thirty-three-and-a-half years.

As Julia continued to listen to my explanation, I stated, "The Scriptures tell us that Jesus did not really **perform** His Christness until He died without sinning, without His having sinned. We know He was **tempted** over and over. Like us, He was tempted twenty-four hours a day. He was aware of Mary Magdalene as a female. He was aware of her just as you or I might be aware of an attractive person in our lives. He was aware of her adoration, the warmth and softness of her touch, of her pleasant odor as she dried His feet with her hair (I'm opening ground for Julia to bring up her present attraction to the man who isn't her husband). And, He was tempted. But temptation isn't sin. Jesus could be tempted, but He alone of all humans, did not sin."

Among her problems, Julia doesn't understand the difference between temptation and sin, her main symptom—unrealistic and un-Christian guilt feelings are, in the end, a defense against the acknowledgment of her own humanness. It is toward that acknowledgment in an emotionally deep way that each of us continuously needs to be reminded and it is this reminder, in a brand-new kind of way, that I am working with here.

"So, we all understand that Jesus could have sinned at any point when He was humanly alive, but He didn't. Had He sinned, He could not possibly have become the Christ. How you and I can't perform perfection, can we?"

"Excuse me, I know I can't; can you?"

I leave it at this point for now. In the itic process with this patient, Julia is just beginning, in fact, to digest the concept. As with other patients who have travelled through this process, none, moreover, have answered "Yes" at that question of whether or not we can perform perfection. They may not have learned to manage their narcissistic element yet—the narcissistic perfection—but they have come to realize, at least, that they really are **not** in control. It is **that** realization which can lead them back to the distinction between who we are and Who God is, back to God's having all Power, and the other key concepts and words that are parts of the whole which make up the theoretical construct for psychiatric practice from a Christian frame of reference. In other words, a Christian Psychiatry.

"MARY JANE"

Anxiety, Depression, Low Self-Worth, Fear/Phobia, Sin Nature

Depression is a problem that involves the Christian psychiatrist with the Christian patient in many of the basic ideas we have been considering. Naturally, it demands that the treatment be Christian in major ways. That means that the whole approach is conditioned by an understanding of the spiritual essence of man and of the patient's original experience of salvation through Jesus. It also, as we shall see, implicates the complex understanding of all aspects of the personality (body, mind, and spirit in their many facets and wholeness). The following case of Mary Jane illustrates these facts.

Mary Jane is a Christian in her fifties who describes herself when she comes to my office thus: "I've been married for twenty-two years. My husband is a good man; we're okay financially. Nothing big, but it is okay. The kids are teenagers—and they **are** teenagers—but they're not terrible. Yet, I just don't have any patience with them now. I'm just so irritable all the time and I feel terrible always biting their heads off. Lately, I've felt like just sitting down and crying, and even do, but many times I don't even know why. All I know is I'm angry all the time. I'm worn out. I just don't care anymore. I'm always tired. I'm not sleeping at all. I've got no energy. I could care less if we ever had sex again or not. In fact, I've been tempted to just leave, just take off! They'd all probably be better off without me anyway the way I am now. I'd rather go to my room and just be left alone."

People with these and other symptoms of depression are seen in every psychiatrist's office every day. Other symptoms might be loss of appetite with weight loss or just the opposite of overeating and weight gain. There may be a sense of confusion and difficulty making decisions with a loss of ability to concentrate or remember things. A sleep disturbance may be difficulty falling asleep because the mind just won't close down or it may be early awakening and not being able to go back to sleep. Or, as with Mary Jane, there can be feelings of worthlessness, uselessness, guilt, being unlovable, or unacceptability.

If the condition worsens, either due to continued and deepening unrecognized maladaptive defensiveness or some other mental, emotional, or immaterial and non-physical process, a biochemical imbalance takes place in the brain cells.[61] This begins to

---

[61] A strict biological psychiatrist, who has no room in his or her understanding such as this of human nature, would put this statement in reverse order, from the position being that the physical, material brain is the non-physical, immaterial mind. God says differently, as I have presented throughout this work.

move into what is called major depression with psychosis. There can be movement from anger to fury to rage with an impulse to action with suicidal and even homicidal ideation. There may be visual and/or auditory hallucinations, i.e., the person may see and/or hear things that no one else sees or hears. Though what they see or hear is not actual, they **experience** it as real. This is why it's so difficult to deal with. If you happen to be around someone like this, it's useless and perhaps detrimental to say, "It's just in your head or in your imagination." It's better to somehow communicate that you understand that what they are seeing or hearing is real to them in that they are experiencing it, but also reassure them that it's "just" symptoms of the illness and they can get better with treatment. This, of course, is usually more effective with someone who has had more than one or two such episodes, maybe, and has previously acknowledged it and sought medication.

Mary Jane's case demonstrates two common dysfunctional symptoms: **anxiety**, the most common dysfunctional symptom of human experience, and **depression**, the most common clinical condition seen in almost any healthcare worker's office. Both of these conditions are preceded by stress that is humankind's biological and psychological destiny. Because of our finiteness, our limitedness, we are destined to experience frustration. That is, that I cannot have exactly what I want, precisely when I want it, not even just because I want it and, therefore, from my standpoint, deserve it. The moment there is a fraction of delay in time or space, I am immediately aware at some level of myself of my limitedness, my finiteness, my impotence, and my vulnerability to harm and destruction. This produces stress which can easily become anxiety at a certain level and, as Rado said it early on in the development of understanding psychodynamics, there results frustration anger. All this relates back to our Theoretical Construct Cornerstone previously outlined in Chapter 2.

All power—unlimitedness—belongs to God. Time and space are of no consequence to Him. He created them and therefore is not subject to them. The only person who can have exactly what He wants, right precisely when He wants it, and without a fraction of a moment's delay is God. He can have it just because **He** wants it, and, in fact, because **He** deserves it.

What a bitter pill to swallow! That's what the sin nature is all about. There really is, in fact, that part of me (and of you) that wants and is looking for a means of not being frustrated. This quest is necessarily, of course, to not be limited, but instead, to have power. This kind of thinking draws the conclusions that the attainment of power is tantamount to being unlimited, and therefore, allows me to have what I want, when I want it, just because I want it, and, of course, since I deserve it. I should and expect to receive it with no cost or effort to me. This is why the sin nature believes in magic. It (the sin nature) must hold this belief because that's what it would take to achieve the impossible.

So, my narcissistic sin nature **operates** 24 hours a day and will as long as I'm in this body desiring and starving for power contrary to God's will. That desiring and striving to distort and/or deny reality is what I term one's maladaptive effort to try and escape the truth. But, again here, we must pray asking God to remind us that the truth shall make us free. We must ask Him to help us to come to understand, and therefore, to willfully accept this truth. Embracing this understanding and His acceptance, there is really no bitter pill at all to swallow to surrender to His one and only deity in Jesus Christ. That it's in the very unlimited omnipotence of Himself and in the very fact that we creatures, even with all our scientific knowledge and technological capabilities, can't get out beyond the magnitude of His scope that our very salvation rests. Again, thank God for the hope that's in Christ Jesus.

Now, let's return to Mary Jane, our fifty-ish, married mother of two teenagers whose socioeconomic circumstances would seem to fit what many would call "all they'd want out of life." But we must remember that God has formed our whole personality structure in a holistic manner with each element interacting with the other in an orgasmic way in which we're alive in this world. The non-material, non-physical elements (the spirit and the mind) are "housed" in and have physical, material representations in the organic substrate of our brain and the other organs of our body. When Mary Jane's frustration stress gained a certain degree through her psycho-neuro-immunological system, it registered to her as anxiety. The anxiety then reached the organic and orgasmic state of depression.

To whatever extent Mary Jane's move toward depression was an unconscious defensive maneuver against anxiety or whatever other psychodynamic purposes the depression might serve for her, one of the first interests of any psychiatrist with a depressed patient is to determine if the organism, in its effort to avoid further anguish, is in danger of attempting to end its own existence.

So, I asked Mary Jane, quite early in our first session: "You stated you've actually cried when you feel this way. Have you ever gotten so down in the dumps that you've just wanted to put an end to it all?"

"Yes," she said, reluctantly, but with relief at her admission with me and at the implicit understanding which I was extending to her.

"Have you ever attempted suicide?"

"No, I haven't."

Then, I pushed toward the reality at the bottom of the feeling and put it to the patient's fundamentals: "Do you want to die?"

Like most patients, Mary Jane said, "No" at this point.

"I did want to die, but I forced myself away from that feeling," she continued.

As her doctor, I needed to know the answer to the next question, not only as an inquiry into her state of mind, but also as a means of preparing the ground of a therapeutic intervention.

"Are you going to kill yourself?"

Some patients might say, "I don't really know" or "not at the moment." Both of these are serious responses, the second perhaps moreso. With either response, I would move into evaluating the possible need for hospitalization, especially if there was evidence of a specific plan and means.

Mary Jane, like most people, said: "No," and had no such plan.

That's what I expected in her case and I replied: "I'm really glad to hear that."

Then I went on, as I typically do with patients in her situation and state of mind: "It would be such a waste. And it would be so unnecessary. And I wouldn't be sure but that you would be jumping from the frying pan into the fire."

Here, I stopped and let her get the full effect, as a Christian, of what issues I have raised. [I am not proposing to state here that everyone who commits suicide automatically will go to hell. Only God can judge their heart. This is a theological question which is beyond the scope of this book. However, I would not hesitate to discuss it as part of the case material in the office.]

What I have done with the Lord's sovereign intervention is moved the whole matter into a spiritual, biblical, Christian frame of reference. I have said that I would hate her suicide because it would be a human waste. I have asserted her personal value to me and her objective value in the world. I've expressed to her my concern, my "love" for her in a Christian sense. Also, when I said, "so unnecessary," I was also implying there may be alternatives and gave her hope, and indirectly asserted that something could be done about her situation.

One can see how I have been in the process, then, of building a therapeutic alliance. But I go further along the track of a Christian understanding of God's Design of Theory of Personality again, as stated in Chapter 1.

I said at some point, "You know, Mary Jane, if a person has just got to kill herself, there really isn't a thing in the world anybody can do about it. Oh, we could capture you and put you in the hospital and even hold you for three to four weeks or months, even, and hopefully, you'd change your mind. But you know the reality is that you might even figure a way to do it right there in the hospital or, potentially, just bide your time until right after you got out. If a person has just got to die, that's that person's decision. That's your decision, because only you have the power of **your choices**."

Right here, I was beginning to attach the notion that the "patient" is only that, a passive sufferer, a creature of destiny, of determinism whether inner or outer. I was reminding Mary Jane that she was created with freedom of choice, and therefore, was responsible for her choices, ideas with which, as a Christian, she had some real acquaintance.

Then, I returned to my original reaction and reiterated it by saying, "I'm really glad to hear you're not going to kill yourself" (calling "a spade a spade").

I have reinforced the strength and correctness of her decision by supporting the freedom of her will and sense of individuality, the reality of personal responsibility. Then, I went further using her Christian beliefs, the ones that she carries in the spiritual/ mental part of herself.

"You remember God's sixth commandment, 'Thou shalt not kill' (Exodus 20:13; Deuteronomy 5:17; Matthew 5:21; Romans 13:9 KJV). The NAS and NIV render the better translations of these scriptures which mean, 'Thou shalt not murder.' This is more accurate because God isn't talking about not killing animals or even other people under certain circumstances. If someone is trying to rape your child and the only way you can stop him is by killing him, I know of nothing in the Bible that prohibits shooting him. That's not murder. It's killing, but not murder, neither legally nor morally. In fact, it may be a sin not to do so.

Moving along, I state, "But suicide is murder. It's murder of one's own self. But our lives don't belong to ourselves. They belong to God."

"Now, consider with me, Mary Jane: If you or somebody else were to commit suicide, who would have won the battle, God or Satan?"

I let her wrestle with that question—one like many of the interventions I made with Mary Jane that I typically use with depressed Christian patients—until she could see there was but one answer.

I stated, "Satan would have won the battle. And **he** would not even have had to win it, I would have just **given** it to him."

I drove further toward her recognizing that the devil "cannot and never has made anyone do anything." And, in fact, "neither has the Lord." I stated flatly that He "has given us free will."

Most lay Christians will readily agree that we are given free will. But if there is some theological block—a Calvinist theology taken seriously, for instance, by the patient—I'll deal with that theologically. I cite scripture and interpret God's Word for them to bolster the natural sense of free will that Christians have, whatever their theology. I had to do this with Mary Jane.

"Now, Mary Jane, we know from scripture that God is all powerful. So, He could violate our free wills if He wanted to. But He says over and over that He would not **be** God—generous and loving in the highest—if He were to do that. So, our free will is God-given. The adversary, on the other hand, would violate our free will if he could, but he doesn't have the power, as we know from what we've discussed and based on the Word. So, Mary Jane, the Holy Spirit appeals to me and you, and on the other hand, the un-holy spirit also appeals to me and to you. But only you and I have the power to choose which one each of us is going to respond to."

"Sometimes, however, Dr. Lew, I feel so bad that I just know Jesus will forgive me if I put an end to it all."

"Mary Jane, there is a theological point you are making here. You are coming from the realization, perfectly correct, that once saved, always saved. Once a person has accepted Jesus as Savior, she's saved forever. So, we have to consider whether God would forgive you if you killed yourself. The scripture reveals the ultimate sin is only blasphemy—the denial of God's existence. Because of that, I can indeed imagine if someone were totally confused, dreadfully ill in their state of mind, forced, for example, by physical pain beyond their capacity to think and will—such a person, perhaps, might be forgiven by God as non-responsible, like a child, and as a child might be forgiven."

"Are you, however, in that place, really?"

"No, Doc. Not really in that place."

"Right. You have had classical symptoms of depression: irritation, fatigue, sadness, suicidal ideation, and so on. But not to the point of not knowing right from wrong. You may be indecisive about many things, little things—what to do with the kids on

Saturday when you're feeling so bad, even whether to go to work on a particular day—but any really important decision—a violation of commandments, for instance—you're not there; right?"

"Right. I'm not there."

In speaking to her this way, I was raising symptoms the depressed patient might not even know she had in order to get them out in the open. But I was always containing them within that spoken Christian context to assist in the healing. I was speaking to the unconscious, attending faculty of the mind.

With Mary Jane, like most patients, it took passing over some of the same material several times before she was able to see that she was responsible for her own choices and, moreover, that **I** was not responsible for them, which made fertile ground for us to move forward. We were ready, thus, to move forward. This was a potentially dangerous point in movement—once a depressive begins to feel some renewal of energy and her responsibility for results, she can easily plunge into a new despair, and in fact, actually commit suicide.

So, I made clear again something I had said before: "I can't **make you** *be* 'weller' (I did not say '**make you** *feel* **weller**'). I don't have the capacity to do that. Only you do. Only you have the power of your choices. You're beginning to see that pretty clearly now. I am interested in being of service to you in the ways that I know I can be. My service, though, is primarily to your own effort in coming to understand more about your own personality structure—how you happen to tick the particular way that you do."

Even here in the beginning, in order to move onward to the more analytical aspect of treatment, I was constantly reaffirming her own freedom of will, her ability to choose, and her responsibility.

It's not just the depressed patient who has a tendency continually to forget these things—we all do!

I asked her, "Mary Jane, how is it that you happen to be disturbed by your husband's wanting to go out with his friends on occasion? You have said you feel he's unloving and you feel he might even be cheating on you."

I was bringing back for her consideration what she had stated to me, trying to quote her words back to her verbatim.

"I assume that is part of why you came here—so you can come to understand something more about your own personality structure. You've said that 'jealousy' is one of your problems, for instance, and that it is part of your depression. Those thoughts and feelings you've told me about are not just coming out of the air, but from some level within your own mental functioning. I assume you want to learn more about how you happen to tick so that, hopefully, you can choose to do something differently than what you have been doing."

Like nearly all patients, who sooner or later, with more or less thoughtfulness, reluctance or enthusiasm, come to an assent, Mary agreed.

It is at this point in treatment, sometimes even earlier, that people not infrequently say, "I've had counseling or therapy before, but I've never had anyone talk the way you do."

Usually, they don't know exactly what they mean, but if they can state their meaning, it goes more or less along these lines: "I've never had a psychiatrist say that I am responsible." And, this experience and understanding is always accompanied, oddly, by a sense of relief.

The other thing patients sometimes say in this context is: "You express an understanding of my pain **and** you also assert, in various ways, that you can help and are willing to help. You haven't denied any of my hurt, you accept where I am, and you radiate hope—you say so matter-of-factly: 'it would be so unnecessary to commit suicide.'"

What they are picking up on is some of the basics of Christian psychiatry: a practice informed by a tenaciously-held understanding of our God-given human dignity in free will and of natural hopefulness illuminated by Christian faith in God's promises, the reality of the Spirit within us, the possibility of grace, and so forth. Of course, I radiate hope. Of course, I bolster a patient's sense of this responsibility and potential ability to change. Why? Because I know it's the truth. I know the truth applied is real. I've seen too much of its blessed rewards in my own life as well as in other's lives. Knowing all this, and put quite simply, it would be un-Christian not to.

With Mary Jane, as typically with other patients, the manifested or overt Christian content of our conversations will happen in spurts over the sessions. From this, there will develop a particular clinical point of issue, the evolution of which may be biblically informed, for instance, but I will present biblical principles explicitly and only when I know they fit the therapeutic moment, and will, hence, be most useful. Then we discuss the relevant biblical material for its practical application to the particular patient's point of issue.

"Last visit, Mary Jane, you mentioned that since being in therapy, you've run into the realization that you have another particular problem. You've recognized that you've always had a lot of anxiety and been a chronic worrier. Let's look at what God's Word says in Philippians 4:6-7, 'Do not be anxious about anything, but in everything, by prayer and petition, with thanksgiving, present your requests to God. And the peace of God, which transcends all understanding, will guard your hearts and your minds in Christ Jesus' (NIV). Does that mean you're not to worry, though? Here you are, in your depressive moments, worrying obsessively. Have you ever thought about worrying as a sin?"

"Well, Doc, I've heard that idea before, but I've never really thought about it. I really don't understand it. Why would worrying be a sin?"

"Okay, let's think about it," I suggested followed by a short pause.

"What is worry?" I asked with a longer pause.

"Does it seem perhaps to have something to do with wanting to be in **control**? In control of what's **going** to happen? Trying, searching, yearning, fretting, pushing your mind and feelings as if you could be in control of the future? Whether you'll get the job, arrive safely off a long plane ride, see your child grow up healthy, make enough money, and so forth?"

"I would wonder with you, Mary Jane, whether you or I can actually be in control of the future, regardless of how much we worry about it. In fact, has worry ever been of any practical value to you?"

"Well, yes. I remember, for instance ..."

Mary Jane's example was, of course, flawed. Every time a patient makes such an assertion and gives an example, there is inevitably a flaw. The reason for this inevitability will become apparent as we continue. Sometimes, the patient is confusing rational, realistic planning and rehearsing with worrying. Much more often they are simply expressing the common, and by that I mean the universal, human belief in "Magic"—that we humans can be in control of anything, including the future, is a universal delusion. It is a wishful, frightening, cherished narcissistic fantasy. The fantasy is that they have substantial power over the future or even any control of anything — which is God's all along.

When Magic comes up, I deal with its unreality. Then, I gradually lead them to the sense of balance in living, which the Bible expresses in so many ways, pointing out, as I did with Mary Jane, "Yes, God says don't worry. But does He say have no responsibility and concern for possible future events? For what 'might' happen tomorrow? It's a balance, isn't it? He says, 'You have been given intelligence and judgment by Me. Use these, but don't worry.' God is so reasonable, so down-to-earth, so to speak. Be concerned about tomorrow, but don't be worrying—there's a difference."

Then, typically, as most others do, she asked: "Well, what exactly **is** the difference? In fact, Ecclesiastes 7:16-18 says, 'Do not be over-righteous, neither be overwise—why destroy your-self? Do not be overwicked, and do not be a fool—why die before your time? It is good to grasp the one and not let go of the other. Whoever fears [reveres] God will avoid all extremes [will avoid all extremes keeping everything in balance]' (NIV)."

As a Christian psychiatrist I answered: "Worrying is trying to get over into God's territory. If you think about it, what you're saying is that you're going to put **your *mind*** to it and consider **everything** that could possibly happen. And, if you do these mental acts, the getting into your tomorrows that may never happen, that probably will never happen, and worst-case scenarios, what have you actually accomplished?"

"In the first place, you can't think of everything. That's beyond us and most of the time you're just spinning your wheels—the worst cases are those you can't do anything about; moreover, they usually don't happen. Think about it, how many times have you had the experience of anticipating some dreadful thing about tomorrow—a failure, an accident, a death—and it hasn't happened? If you're the worrier you say you are, you've probably done that literally millions of times, millions of micro-seconds of alternating worries going through your mind and feelings, nano-twinges of worries that never came to pass. So, in all of this, you're responding today as if you were like God—knowing the future, being able to predict that a stone will fall from a rock and the rock will split and move and roll down onto the highway at a certain moment when you're driving and...which is it? Does it hit your car or does it just miss? Or, does the stone not even move because a drop, a single drop of rain falls onto the other side and keeps it balanced? 'God only knows; right?'"

"But what about planning and thinking things through, Dr. Lew, you mentioned something along those lines?"

"**Being concerned** is different. You need to make your mortgage payments, so you think about that and make plans and efforts. You get a job, work, and get money for those payments. You have **concerns** and you act on them with consideration. But you don't worry. It's useless.

God wants us to recognize Who **He** is. **He** is the One in charge. **He** is the One Who is never taken by surprise. And **He** is the One Who wants us to realize that, no matter what takes place tomorrow, **He** will still be in charge—even if **you** lose your house. You don't have to be in charge because, you can't be."

"I'm reminded of Shadrach, Meschach, and Abednego. Nebuchadnezzar said to them: 'If you don't bow down, I'm going to throw you in the fire. They would feel the heat,' he said, and they thought so, too. But they replied, 'We're not going to kneel down, we can't. We must worship the only God—Yahweh. But we want you to understand, even if we burn—and we expect to burn—we must exercise our **faith** in God. Our faith is not that we are not going to burn—our faith is that if **God** chooses that we will not burn, then we won't. Either way, our faith is the same: we know that He is the Power, the Life, the One God, and He is the Lord of all.'"

After such an intervention, and I did this with Mary Jane, I would reinforce the Christian patient's knowledge by saying,

"The object of our faith is not the outcome of a situation—we can pray for such things, of course. Rather, the object of our faith is Jesus and we leave the outcome to Him. How could any result that I and all the wise men of the world might conjure up even begin to measure up to what God Himself would have in mind? In a sense, faith is a trust in this principle of Truth! Jeremiah 29:11 says, 'For I know the plans I have for you,' declares the LORD, 'plans to prosper you and not to harm you, plans to give you a hope and a future' (NIV)."

I also pointed out, "We often look back and think that if we had done such-and-such in our past, things would have been different: I wouldn't have had that car wreck, lost my money, and so forth. There is a fallacy in such thinking, however. If we had indeed taken another route, another choice of career, house, spouse, and so on, we have no idea **whatsoever** what other, perhaps worse disaster might have happened. This is a kind of retrospective worry. Like future worry, it is quite useless. Useless because it is an attempt at the impossible—to put oneself in the position of God, once again—and only God has that 'kind of power' or, more accurately, states has 'power,' simply, to know the future. **We,** you and me, Mary Jane, are limited and the sooner we accept that fact, the less pain we will cause ourselves."

With Mary Jane and with every other patient, whatever else I might be clarifying by way of Christian concepts that apply to particular circumstances, I'm also reinforcing the Christian's belief and sense that God loves them. "God loves you," I will affirm over and over. Often, I will introduce this idea in the very first session. I never wait very long to do so.

And, with Mary Jane, in this intense session about worry, I presented again: "Remember, God says in His Word that He loves us and He proved it at the cross."

She started to cry and said, "I know it's true, but I can't believe it for me. I feel so bad so often. I feel so unworthy."

"But God still **does** love you. Of course, you are unworthy. The fact is, as scripture points out, we're all unworthy." Or, I might say the opposite, depending on the individual patient and his or her immediate situation, "Are you worthy?"

I am sure she thought, "What are you talking about? Don't you know I am hurting? You say you're interested in my welfare, but why are you being so unkind to me?"

I'm pretty sure she's going to have such responses when I say what I do. My aim is to have her recognize, acknowledge, and come to accept that she is, in fact, unworthy before God.

"I'm really not trying to be mean, Mary Jane, I'm just trying to help you to understand that every stinking one of us before God is unworthy."

"What do you mean?" she whispered.

"Are you and I really worthy before God? As I recall, God said through Paul in Romans 3:10 (KJV), 'There is none righteous, no, not one.' If God knows what He is talking about, none of us is worthy, then. God says in Romans 3:23, 'All have sinned, and come short of the glory of God.' Again, in 1 John 1:10: 'If we say that we have not sinned, we make Him a liar, and His Word is not in us' (KJV). One of the things, dear, that you and I have to really come to know deeply is that we are, in fact, **not** worthy."

"Thank God for grace! For that is the only way that you and I can survive in this world. God's mercy is our foundation. If I got what I deserved, what I'm worthy of, I'd go straight to Hell."

At this point with Mary Jane, I did what I have been willing to do with patients when I think it will help put a point across. I theatrically cringed in my seat, held up my hand in a defensive and imploring way, even sank down, and said: "Oh Lord, please don't give me what I am worthy of."

Usually, such a hammy maneuver brings the patient to laughter. They begin to realize that I, the Doctor, am just another fellow pilgrim and that tends to strengthen the therapeutic bond. The most important value, however, is that they also can begin to laugh at themselves. They come to see something they never did before— that they have been taking themselves so very seriously. Their little lives and their little sufferings, in fact, all **our** lives and sufferings are just not so critically significant in the overall scope of things. Significant, yes, but just not critical.

I went on with Mary Jane to reinforce this emerging sense of proportion, trying to get across some adequate notion of God's grace and **Who** He is and **What** He had done for us in coming here in the same physical, material, bodily shape and form as we are. I talked about how He contended with the world in the body and, yet, without sin. How the Son had thereby become worthy, before the Father, **for me and for her**. How God, having taken the punishment for **my** failure, for our failure, has redeemed us.

Not because we were worthy, but because of His grace. Jesus, the man, became **the** Christ, **the** Messiah, **the** Savior, for each of you and me. And it was that process of living sinlessly, "being tempted in all wise as ye and me," and taking the penalty of death onto Himself, willfully, when not even being subject to it, which justifies us before the judgment seat of the One and Only Holy God.

"Worthy? Mary Jane, all we are worthy of is Hell and damnation. Thank God for His grace and the mercy He has shown us. He did that **for** us. It wasn't only three days on the mount that He suffered, He contended for thirty-three-and-a-half years! God, in the flesh, opening Himself to temptation, twenty-four hours a day, yet, without sin. That's God. That's us. All I can do is be thankful."

It's easy to see how such kinds of interventions with Christians, many of whom are neither devout nor engaged in daily or even monthly practice, can gradually help an individual come out of successful treatment with a long-term, life-long foundation for living well without recurrent symptoms, in a way that secular therapy with secular patients cannot offer.

"So now, let me pose the question again, Mary Jane. Are you and I worthy? Is the Pope worthy? Is my dear Christian Mama worthy before God, worthy of God's love? I am reminded of Psalm 8:4: 'What is man that You are mindful of him?'"

"Well, Doc, you've helped me realize that I'm not worthy, and not only that, but why. Also, it's helped tremendously to know that even though that's so—it's okay. So, I certainly have gotten a lot of hope from talking with you. You've reminded me that I am not alone. No matter how bad I feel or how bad, in fact, I am, that I have God's love available to me in Jesus. I have Jesus. You helped me remember."

"RICKY"

OCD, Depression, Perfection, Separation

Among the most common problems which Christian patients specifically present to practitioners is perfectionism. Here, as with all patients, the Christian psychiatrist employs an integral approach that uses all the best techniques of modern medicine and secular therapies in union with Christian theory, principles, and faith. Patients who suffer from perfectionism can be especially moving to the doctor because their lives are so limited, distorted, and pain-ridden because of a distorted understanding of what God demands of them and Who God is. This sort of Christian perfectionism quite naturally develops out of, is all mixed up with, and is colored by childhood histories that can be extremely unhappy.

When a man whom I will call "Ricky" first came to see me, his presenting complaint was a serious depression. Behind that, Ricky had a history of alcoholism, one which he had fought. In trying to self-treat his depression with cocaine, however, he had fallen off the wagon and had finally gone to the hospital to get off crack and alcohol, and to get medical help with his depression. He was referred to me because he stated he went to church regularly, was an active Christian, and I was a Christian psychiatrist.

I first went through the suicide check of the type I had used with Julia, attempting to see how much he was at risk. I could see he was quite depressed, far beyond feeling down in the dumps. He told me he had not only thought about suicide; he had a plan.

"Exactly how would you kill yourself?"

"Driving head-on into an eighteen-wheeler."

"Do you want to die?"

"Sometimes, Doc, I really do."

"Are you going to kill yourself, Ricky?"

"Well, I guess not. I don't feel that way right now. At the moment, I don't really want to die."

I replied to him in a way I have found useful in testing a patient's deeper religious beliefs: "Well, I'm sure glad to hear that—it would be such a waste and it's so unnecessary. But also, I'm not so sure it wouldn't be jumping out of the frying pan right into the fire."

I was watching all along to see his understanding of the scriptures and his sense of his relationship with God. Where was this man spiritually? I needed to find out.

He knew what fire I meant and he believed in its reality. In short, he was the sort of man who, being afraid of God, was afraid of Hell. Under the circumstances, I didn't have to put him on elopement or suicide precautions, so I started him on anti-depressants, put him on the detox service, and we began treatment.

This was a relatively long-term course.

Ricky was thirty-seven years old, married with three children, the eldest being about sixteen. He was a good provider and worked as an expert carpenter and builder, a very skilled craftsman. He was also very active in his church, a deacon, ordained, and helping to run the business of the church. The most striking source of his problems in childhood was his relationship with a very difficult father, a man who beat him frequently and badly, who was angry and unreasonably demanding, unloving, and cold.

As our conversations proceeded, I came quickly to the conclusion that I had a case here of classic Obsessive Compulsive Personality Disorder in a Christian. Not every such person has all of Ricky's characteristics, of course, but many are very common. For one thing, there was revealed the pattern of childhood abuse. Abused children often turn into adults who can't say "No" to the demands of others. They have been taken advantage of in all kinds of ways, sometimes including sexual molestation, and they have come to feel a deep sense they haven't the right to say "No." They don't perceive it to be an option for them. This pattern is most evident with sexually abused females who usually end up with dependent personality or borderline personality features. Although Ricky was not abused in that particular way, he had a strong streak of it.

Not only did he teach a Sunday school class, he was the department head. He helped repair the church on nights and weekends.

He was in the choir. He went to deacon meetings. Anything that anybody needed help with, they knew to call Ricky. He'd be right there.

And, yet, despite all this "churchy" activity, I saw there was not much joy or peace in this man's Christianity.

The rest of his life was filled with the same desolate and cold rage for accomplishment, order, and control.

"I never waste time," he said.

He was always early to an appointment, just a little bit. Everything had to be in its place, he said: his garage, car, and tool chest were all perfectly ordered and clean. His wife and children were strictly enlisted in these efforts: everything had to be done at home his certain way. There was a system for everything, an organization. No surprise to me that his relationships were empty. Ricky seldom expressed feelings of any kind, his wife was cold to him, and he didn't know his sons at all. His private life had a stern military quality.

The relationship with his wife was disappointing, there was little sex after the first years and there was no warmth, tenderness, or affection. She had lost interest. People did what he expected, but out of obligation and duty only. Because of this, any activity—even "churchy" activity—didn't fulfill his emotional needs and he would then fill up with unresolved anger, a sense of being put upon, of being unappreciated, and of self-pity!

Because his Christian beliefs were distorted, he was quite immature spiritually. Despite his "Christian beliefs," Ricky would turn elsewhere in search of the Truth or some resolution. To get some sense of reward, some kind of good feeling, he turned to the alcohol and crack. But these were no solutions for him because their use or outcome was never going to possibly provide to him his needed desire for security any more than it would for any other human.

And, yet, he acted as if he could do the impossible. He even thought he was doing it. Over and over again, he told me that we should do perfection here on earth, in our lives. Gradually, his sense of guilt emerged, over and over, as he tried to do the impossible, to be all things to everyone, and knowing he wasn't succeeding some of the time, and, then, feeling guilt and sadness about that. Gradually, too, I was able to lead him to unearth what was behind those feelings of guilt and then to tell me where all those "shoulds" and "musts" came from in his past, tracing them back to childhood origins. We always got back to his father and that voice, demanding, pressing, and punishing. Each of these acts of connection was a little step in his liberation, his seeing that what was pushing him came from elsewhere, from a past that was not his present. He slowly detached himself from these driving, unconscious compulsions, but only very slowly. For, like many patients, this one was bright, but not a very emotionally available or agile person.

Defensive and difficult to reach, not very well educated, both emotional and intellectual channels were far from flowing for Ricky. The fact that he was so "productive"—cutting out pieces of lumber and dedicated to keeping everything squared up, kept him defended. At the bottom, he didn't have a fear so much of being out of control, his fear was of not being **completely _in_** control!

In the end, such a man's liberation in therapy could only come through clarifying for him—again, repeatedly—the Christian principles to which he was, though unbeknownst to him by the grace of God, dedicated. I took them up, one-by-one, and applied them to his problems and distorted false notions in an attempt to put his perfectionism in true perspective. These opportunities came in bits and pieces, whenever he was ready to hear. Early on that was mostly when he was suffering, vulnerable, and open or— for whatever reasons and circumstances—clear-minded.

One main thing we had to work on was his largely unconscious and contradictory image of God. Even though he had his personal relationship with Christ and was, thereby, saved, it was clear that he was ever **working** for his salvation, without even knowing it. In other words, he didn't really believe in or understand God's grace. He felt that he had to be busy earning, achieving, measuring up, doing, and doing perfectly what had already been granted. For him, God was not a loving and caring being, but rather a punitive one: an "I'm-going-to-get-you" kind of god. When Fowler and others talk about this sort of belief, they see it as belonging to a childish stage of faith. Indeed, Ricky the perfectionist had imported this vision of God from his experience with his own punitive father. The way a child sees their father can influence their sense of God and, frequently in Christian psychiatry, we have to help the patient adjust this childish carryover with what he already knows as an adult to be a more accurate image of God.

This psychological habit pattern of reaction, like any other, doesn't give place to new ones easily.

"Ricky, the Bible says that 'to fear the Lord is the beginning of wisdom.' Are you afraid of God?"

"I guess so. All the time, really."

"You remember, we talked about that a few sessions ago. Why do you think the scriptures would ask us to be afraid of God when we know He is so full of love for us, He gave His Son for us, He gives us the grace for faith, and so on, and He tells us to **love** Him and to **love** one another? And, what does it mean that 'perfect love driveth out all fear?' There seems to be an apparent contradiction, does it not?"

"Yes," he answered, musing and wondering. "But I can't make sense of it."

"A better translation of the verse, 'to fear the Lord is the beginning of wisdom' is 'to revere the Lord is the beginning of wisdom.' It is a sense of reverence that is being evoked. To be reverent is to be in awe. 'To be awed by the Lord is the beginning of wisdom.' Doesn't that make sense out of the apparent contradiction between fear and love? What it means is recognizing the relative insignificance of ourselves like when people speak of being 'awed' by the Grand Canyon. It seems, perhaps, that in our Christianity it is the splendor, the beauty, the implied power, the greatness, the very magnitude of the Lord—What and Who God is in relationship to our puny dimensions—that is the point?"

"Well," he said, reflecting, "I see what you're saying."

"If we focus on that 'awe'-fullness, that 'awe'-worthiness of God, if we remind ourselves that all those qualities apply to His love for us, a **sense of something else** begins to emerge. It seems you've been very afraid of God and I'm just not aware of any scripture that says 'be ye **afraid** of God.'"

I was beginning to try and recall him to, to reconstruct for him, and make it preponderant, the God he knew of as an adult, but Who was not allowed to rule his life.

God's grace was a recurrent theme in the moments when I could intervene with him on this religious level.

Once I challenged him: "Can you get an abutment perfectly squared?"

"Yes, I can get it perfectly square," he affirmed, somewhat to my astonishment.

Like most of us, he didn't realize that perfect was just not possible; even if the angle was functionally straight, for example, it would be subject to change. I talked to him about that — "When we have done all we can do"—and here I would switch from the physical to emotional or the mental realm—"it's not perfect."

"We cannot think perfectly nor love perfectly. There is an element of the church that teaches agape love, but there is not even a single human being who can do such pure agape love. If they could, Jesus didn't have to die for them. Only God can love that way."

I would get at all these truths with all the craft and eloquence in my possession. I reminded him of our dependence, our limitedness, showing him that his perfectionism was an utterly unreasonable attempt to be God Himself. The sacrifice of Jesus is the measure both of God's love and our powerlessness to overcome sin. Slowly, Ricky began to get clear in his mind and also feel in his gut, in his emotional structure and in his body, that he alone couldn't overcome his sin nature. He recognized the magnitude of his personal and complete helplessness to not sin. He felt inside himself, more and more, the dimension of what God had done for him: God coming into the world, in the same human condition as Ricky, subject to the same temptations, feelings, and limitations, yet in perfect faith, in utter righteousness, choosing the personal relationship with the Father and faith in the Father Who said: "I will take unto Myself, through My Son whom I love, for sinners everywhere, the consequences of sin." In Luke 22:44, it says Jesus went through this emotional, sweating-blood torment for us. Then the whole cycle was finished—everything from the garden, the fall, the patriarch, the prophets, and the gift of the Holy Spirit. Ricky came to understand and feel that God had done it thoroughly—the salvation of humankind by grace and divine sacrifice.

Over and over, I had to appeal to his conscious intelligence to revise his childish fears. We talked about Paul's "thorn in his side," for instance. No one knows what the thorn was exactly, but Paul prayed three times to be relieved of it. In essence, God was saying you need this thorn, this imperfection. We need our imperfections to help us remember that God said, "My grace is sufficient, and My strength is made perfect, fulfilled, in your weakness." I showed Ricky, to his satisfaction, that when I accept my weakness and adopt a submissive attitude before God, I immediately open my spirit and my daily living to the love and power of the Almighty.

"That is why, Ricky, people who live according to these precepts seem to be able to bear the normal problems of living so much more easily than others. That's why, so often, God intervenes in more particular ways which Christians describe as 'miracles.' Don't you know radiant, happy people in your church who are like that?"

He nodded as it set him thinking.

Over and over, we got to his father's voice, the source of his punishing perfectionism. And, again and again, I exposed to him the irrationality, the absurdity of a Christian operating under these unrealistic burdens of perfectionism. In fact, unusually, he wasn't consciously aware that he actually meant and tried to live out this unreasonable and un-Christian perfectionism. For example, one day he began to feel guilty and angry because his wife wanted him to go to a PTA meeting for the children and the preacher in his church wanted him to go to a deacon's meeting.

After talking about his dilemma a bit, he began to experience a basic clarity: "I can't be in two places at once."

"Right, and you don't, therefore, have to be. You're not a bad person if you can't be, you're not inadequate, neglectful or unloving because you can't do the impossible. You're just a human being; like everyone else; limited; so rest in the perfection of God."

"Okay. I'll just leave perfection to God then."

My job, over time, was to help him understand as described above that nothing terrible would happen if he, for instance, didn't get an angle **absolutely** square. One aspect of perfectionism is seeing things in "either/or" terms, *absolutely*. There are no grays, no middle ground—it's all either good or bad. Living on these assumptions leads to a painful lack of balance. There is and can be no poise or equilibrium with or understanding that there is such a thing as "enough." This precious knowledge, once gained, is that which allows a person to feel and be balanced in his attitudes and actions (cf. Ecclesiastes 7:16-18). Once a person understands about "enough," he can go on and understand that there can be "too much"—put another way, what was a strength (purposeful, conscientious effort) can become a hindrance.

Such abstractions are obvious in their truth, the hard part is getting them home in a meaningful way. With Ricky, I had to work with him to understand, recognize, acknowledge, and accept *the reality of his actually having **no** control*. I told him about the man who tried to kill himself in vain because God wasn't ready for that. I had to reawaken his sense of God's grandeur and our complementary smallness to Him, of God's generosity, of His love, and of His gift of our salvation as Christians. Further, I had to make real the spiritual truths he had already experienced, but which were eclipsed by the ingrained effects of his upbringing and habits.

Gradually, it worked. He began to accept his own Christian viewpoint as reality and to say such things as "I can rest in the perfectness of God" to himself. He began to **prioritize**, an essential step for an Obsessive-Compulsive, and to become a better steward of his talents, his time, his opportunities, and his personhood.

Becoming more and more consciously aware of the emotional and behavioral habit patterns he'd developed in early childhood, he stated, "A little red flag goes up now and I'm reminded I've been down that path before! I really do know that it always leads to something different."

When he reacted as he had earlier, he would catch the maladaptive emotional and behavioral patterns developed in early childhood.

"A little red flag goes up, Dr. Lew, and it has written on it: 'Stop and think this over.'"

Because in our work he'd learned to use the circle diagram depicting the Psychology of Conversion, he would also be aware of the little dot in the center of the circles reminding him: "I am not God and I am nothing without God, but I'm okay," and that's acceptance. That's growth!

Ricky became less narcissistic and less prideful, however unconscious his pride had been. He found more and more peace in his own being—still limited, less than perfect, and therefore, needful of God's grace. In time, he was able to translate his vertical relationship to God and to bring it into his relationship with all the people around him. In a word, he became more loving, more radiant, patient, and joyful. These are all the rewards of accepting grace. At home, he slept better.

His wife was amazed and told me: "He's not withdrawn all the time. He talks. He plays with our children—**plays**. People like him now, not just for what he can do for them, but just because they like to be with him."

Crucial to the warming of this rigid, self-driving, and cold man were the occasions when he could allow himself to break through to his emotional nature. There was one period, for example, when I had been working on helping him to come to some forgiveness for his abusive father. He had said he would never be able to forgive what had been done to him by that brutal man. Then, one day, he suddenly became very quiet. In the session before this one, I had prompted him to ask himself if his father had ever done anything good for him. Ricky's chin began to tremble after these minutes of quiet.

"What are you feeling? Whatever it is, you can feel it, you can even tell me if you choose to."

"I don't want to cry," he said, stiffening. "I don't want to get emotional."

This is an important point with a great many Christian patients who, so often, are more or less perfectionistic.

"But Ricky, my friend, isn't that what we are doing here... trying to get to feelings, your emotional life? And didn't Jesus cry? Didn't Jesus have all sorts of emotions? And if He did, it's okay, perfectly okay, for me and you, isn't it?"

Before my eyes, he made a conscious, willful decision to recall the incident fully. And he told me how his dreadful father had come to his high school graduation, apparently trying to acknowledge an "achievement" for the boy who was never "good enough."

Again, we sat in silence.

Then Ricky finally spoke: "I guess he really loved me."

Then his tears and sobs came. It was extraordinary to see this in such a man who always had wanted to be "**in** control." His face became wet, the hands covering them were wet, the knees of his pants were wet. In that moment, he began to forgive his father because he realized there had been, despite all the abuse, something else. Out of that deeply felt realization, not just an intellectual appreciation, the anger and resentment sides of his own lack of self-worth became a cold thaw. This incident, a product of a long trajectory of coming into greater self-knowledge, influenced his self-esteem. And, it also influenced his understanding of what he was not giving his own sons—the love needed to establish a healthy self. It was after this that he began to become less harsh and demanding and more forgiving, more accepting of his own fallibility and of his humanness. There began to develop a new freedom to recreate himself —not according to his father's punitive mode.

Two further notes: the long-term follow-up and the long-term economic benefits of such treatment in a case like Ricky's where the ways of feeling, thinking, and acting acquired and solidified in nearly four decades of living have to be changed and transcended. Ricky did fine over the long term. He continued his evolution over the five years or so that I saw him for annual check-ups, after the initial nearly two years of intensive treatment.

His wife, unfortunately, didn't do so well herself with Ricky's changes. However, though, Ricky's coping with her divorcing him three years after he first came to see me only served to show how far he had come. She had never come in for therapy herself, and though I had met her, she never asked for help. She was starting to get a man who was beginning to be able to love her and be considerate to her. But she chose to get out, she turned on him like a viper, demanded more than her share, and got it.

It was probably a mistake on her part, a precipitous decision once her fear of him subsided because he was becoming softer. It's too bad that she couldn't have turned to God, the church, the Christian community, or a Christian psychiatrist, rather than bolting. Christians should use all their means to put such moments of life panic or life hurt, in a rational and Christian perspective. That can be a long process, but we must try to reach out if we possibly can. On the other hand, it may be that no help would have been effective and that it was healthy, certainly, for the woman to be self-assertive, self-empowering. The price, however, that she and the rest of the family paid, was very high.

When she demanded everything—furniture, car, truck, bank account—Ricky was, amazingly, able to forgive her. He had reached that point. Not at first but a few months afterwards: "If she wants to do that, I can live with it." About six months after I had last seen him professionally, I was having dinner in a restaurant and noticed Ricky seated in a booth by himself, dressed in coat and tie. A few minutes later, a stylish woman walked in and approached him. He gave her a big hug, his face lit up, and they chatted all through the dinner in a very comfortable way. He's survived, moved on, and he'd done it by becoming a much better

Christian and therefore, a healthier, more flexible, warmer, and caring person.

What is important to notice here is this "conversion," so to speak, of a rigid scowler into an effective loving man was through time and many hours of help using strictly Christian theoretical principals, professionally organized.

Christian psychiatrists must worry how this sort of long-term and necessarily expensive treatment can be paid for under our present system of insurance. I saw Ricky once a week for nearly two years. The insurance company didn't see the necessity of that, so I had to make a heavy personal contribution to the expense of Ricky's treatment. The company wanted symptom relief. It would pay only for the lifting of the depression. It had no interest in making Ricky a better or more loving person, someone less obsessively perfectionistic.

That's a false economy, however, derived from a false notion of economics. Realizing the goal for a human being of becoming more balanced, more loving, a better father, a better husband, a person less likely to have physical and mental breakdowns, one who won't again be hospitalized, one who will go to work regularly and not take time off because of depression or anxiety, who will be more effective because he is not tormented by feelings of meaninglessness, whose home is peaceful, whose kids aren't likely to become juvenile delinquents—that's expensive in the short run but cheap over time.

The Christian community has to find a way to make appropriate long-term treatment available, not only in the interest of the individual patient, but for the good of the society which he will inevitably affect in innumerable ways.

"KATHY AND TOM"

Power (God's), Security, Iceberg, Codependency, Narcissism, Abandonment, Neurosis, Psychosis

Consider the wife whose husband wants dinner ready when he gets in from work at 5:30 and she's trying to get it prepared for him because she loves him, and he loves her. But as she works, she holds the four-month-old on her hip who is wanting to nurse, the two-year-old is over climbing on the bookshelf which is about to tip over, and the telephone rings while the doorbell is buzzing. If she would just go ahead and magically exercise her "power" and be all things to all these people, all at once, that would be great. Wouldn't it? Except that there's one thing which goes with that if it were so. She would also be guilty, then, if she didn't perform all that because if she didn't, her belief that she can be God—her narcissism—tells her she could and therefore, she should. What foolishness not to surrender to the truth. There's an old adage which states that *each time we try to disprove a principle of truth, we do nothing but prove it.*

As a therapist I have responsibility toward the patient—I deeply know this—but I cannot be responsible **for** the patient. This is way beyond my "power." Here, there is a similarity to a good parent: parents have a responsibility toward their children but can never be responsible **for** their children (i.e. their choices). They may have legal responsibilities for the effects of those choices, but no responsibility for their choices. How could they? Similarly, if as a therapist I am operating under the fallacious belief in the power of magical thinking, then I might well feel responsible **for** a patient's choices, the outcomes, and whether he or she kills them self or doesn't "get 'weller'" than when he or she came in. I will feel all is my "fault."

This dangerous attitude is diametrically opposed to the fact of any other person's actual individual and separate existence. I can **never override that human reality!** I am myself limited, I have no magic, I have no power. I can only try to help and be of service. I can't do **for** or **to** the patient—she is responsible for herself. I can only contribute. **Alone.** I cannot determine the outcome. I often say this to patients: "I cannot do it **to** you. I cannot do it **for** you. I can only assist you in **your own efforts** to 'get 'weller'." Here we come back to the most basic truth in the whole structure of Christian psychiatry —God has all power. One sees this reality in every aspect of practice, including questions of right relationship and the separateness of individuals.

A case that illustrates many of these points is that of Kathy and Tom, a married couple with whom I worked. She came first, with a variety of complaints—anxiety, depression, fatigue, and even some symptoms of dissociation. In the very first session, she gave me the basic clue to an underlying level of her problem. I asked her if we could meet at another hour the next week. As many spouses will do, she said she'd have to ask her husband and get back to me about scheduling matters. That was normal enough, but she said this very timidly, even abjectly: "I'll have to see what Tom wants to do."

By the end of the second session, it became clear that she had to ask Tom's "okay" for almost everything. These are dynamics typical of co-dependent couples. She wasn't the only one in the thrall. Naturally, Tom was on the hook, too. He had to be there to provide the answer to every question, to be strong, to be knowing, and so on. In short, both these people had gotten themselves into a way of living where they were denying the basic human separateness and the basic responsibility in living their lives that is sine qua non (absolutely essential) of human dignity.

I worked mainly with Kathy, though I got to see Tom later. As her childhood history emerged in our work together, the origins of her dependent personality pattern became clear. She was driven by the fear and abandonment from her earliest years. The mother had preferred another sibling to a degree that crippled Kathy's sense of her worth. The sister was everything good, Kathy everything medi-ocre; the mother gave presents to the sister, Kathy got nothing; even in the present day, the mother would give handsome and expensive presents to the sister's kids and nothing or tokens to Kathy's children. This deferential pattern regarding gifts was only one of many such dramatic expressions of preference, or from the other side—rejection. I checked with the husband to make sure that Kathy had represented this family background accurately and he corroborated her account.

From such treatment as a child, Kathy developed the terrible fear of abandonment that she manifested in the consulting room and with her husband. She had not been provided the opportunities that mature a sense of positive relatedness that could lead to adult individuation. When I say that *people are separate*, I don't for a moment mean that they don't have relatedness or that those relations don't range in significance from some degree of importance all the way to some even being essential for proper psycho-sexual development. You can't have in childhood, for example, a sense of identity without having been at least valued and hopefully loved. It's a part of what leads to the development of a sense of separate "okay-ness." Kathy's whole life, during childhood and after, became a search for that affirmation.

By the time I first saw her, she had projected the fulfilling of that need for affirmation onto Tom. In fantasy and outside of her awareness, he became psychologically, therefore, essential to her sense of survival. She believed she needed his love for her to have value. More deeply, she was sure that he was the source of her very sense of individual identity and being. Emotionally, Kathy was relating to her husband—she was thirty-two at the time—as if she were a very small child and he was her mother, the good mother she never had. As long as she could have his approval, she would not be abandoned, rejected, humiliated, or thrown away. And, if he ever showed the slightest cloud in his face, she couldn't bear it and would plunge into tears, pleading, present-giving (ironically), and every sort of compliant and abject behavior.

Though part of him hated all of that and complained about it, another part of his unconscious emotional makeup was, in its turn, dependent on her very sense of her need of him. This part elicited the feeling that **he** fulfilled the fantasy. So, paradoxically, even when he was trying to help her change and was in the position of the healthy one—the strong and whole person—her pathology fulfilled the narcissistic sense of omnipotent goodness that he felt the need for and was striving for within his own pathology.

Kathy and I worked together for well over two years. You don't overnight bring light into such darkness, healing into such illness, or create new patterns of thought, feeling, and action in such a life. There was a malignant arrangement between the two of them, a silent and unconscious conspiracy that can be terribly dangerous. The magazine LIFE presented a case story many years ago before we knew so much about co-dependency. It told of a man who had beaten his wife to the point of mutilation, not once but many times. The picture showed her nose squashed to one side, fractured bones, and she'd had to have reconstructive surgery not once but several times. And, finally, he murdered her daughter. Why had she not long ago left him?

Fortunately, Kathy and Tom had not yet gotten anywhere near that point. They might never have, but the tenacity with which co-dependents cling to their patterns is clear: Kathy felt dependent on Tom's approval. Such a dependence to the degree that she believed her life would have no meaning without it and **as if** her life literally depended on it.

Gradually, as Kathy began to do some of the needed psychological work (seeing and acknowledging her childhood situation and the ways she was reenacting it with her husband, among other insights) and emotional work (experiencing anew the deprivation she had felt in the past and the shame she felt for being so abject now—hurts leading to catharsis and, also, a healthy anger), she began to work through some of what Freud would call her "fixations." She began to have a greater sense of separateness and individuality and to accept the Truth and Real-ity more. And, further, she began to be okay with that. She also began to recognize her own limitedness, powerlessness, and her need for God. She recognized that it was God, in fact, Who was the only Being capable of providing security. Only God could provide her that which she sought so desperately and at such a frightening price.

The ultimate ground for her emerging sense of separateness developed through her awareness in tandem with the psychological and emotional work. I would offer her theological insights, backed by the **felt** evidence of my own faith and by recalling hers to herself. I was not concerned about stressing specific interpretations of the Christian message to her because, in her case, what needed to be said was so fundamental that all Christians can agree on it at once. The more she became aware of her dependency wishes, for instance, and of her dependency needs, the easier it was for this emerging, free person to "attach" her "self" to the God she already believed in.

Once we had looked at those dependency "needs," for instance, I could put those in a Christian perspective for Kathy. I reminded her that we have very few real **needs**—meaning "something vital to our basic survival," for that is what **needs** are about. Water is a need. Food is a need. Too many psychiatric theorists and too many ordinary people in our society confuse needs with wants. Most so-called "needs" are illusory, distorted identifications of the ego that are simply not essential. We easily confuse our wants with our needs and are easily driven by false "needs" masquerading and sensed as real or actual. St. Augustine, in *The Confessions*, has long lists of these "falsa bona": fame, friendship, money, feeling wanted, and so on.

Kathy and I, as Christians, could agree that the only need of humankind for "survival" is God in Christ. If I am a Christian, somewhere back in my being, I know that. But knowing is not enough, "Those believest that there is one God. That thou doest well. The devils also believe, and tremble" (James 2:19 KJV). I must also accept the sinless life, the sacrificial, atoning death, and the bodily resurrection of Jesus. As a Christian, I accept and acknowledge the demonstration of "survival" of death!

This is the actual demonstration of that same characteristic of God which is the cornerstone of coming to understand Who and What He is. POWER. Who is He? POWER. What is He? POWER. That same which is the Creation Power is the Resurrection Power. That which demonstrates proof positive of its POWER to fulfill, totally, any and every need or degree thereof for my security per se. [It is that same POWER which infuses my spirit, my very being, to cause me to trust with the whole of me: body, soul (mind), and spirit to the other characteristics amalgamated with the POWER.]

That is, to apply it to all sorts of mundane experiences in the world, relationships, and all, by "faithing." Such faith is without a doubt an act of my will, but made possible by the grace of God. The more nearly I do this, the less distortion or denying of the truth I do. That is to say, the more Real-ity-oriented I am in life, then the more free I therefore feel.

"And ye shall learn the truth, and the truth shall make you free" (John 8:32 KJV). "If the Son therefore shall make you free, ye shall be free indeed" (John 8:36 KJV).

Kathy questioned, "What? How can that be? Especially when I feel so bad about myself? I say with my mouth that I know the truth and if I do and call myself a Christian, why do I feel this way?"

I responded, "It seems that at some level of your mental functioning you believe, as mentioned earlier, in magic. Remember, magic is the desire for and the striving for knowledge and power contrary to God's will. For you to have some power would take some kind of magic, wouldn't it? Since 'all power belongs to God?'"

Kathy answers, "I guess so."

"Yes!" I respond with punctuation and further state, "Well, since **you** have imputed to Tom the capacity to make you be secure — and he's only human just like you and me — **you** imputed power, then, to him. You must believe, then, that you have some to give to him. If the power that you believe he has to give you security comes from you and you have been dependent on him for it as demonstrated by your worshipful behavior in your relationship with him, it seems to me that you actually are worshipping yourself!"

It took a little while, but soon she was able to begin to absorb all this and thereby recognize, then acknowledge, and lastly, accept the truth of the matter. Accepting truth is what it's all about. The evidence of acceptance is that change takes place. *It's what every living one of us has the most trouble with.* But God says the Truth shall make you free. So, as a Christian, she began to see proper context for viewing this dynamic of her personality in her marriage. She began to be able to face the reality of her own narcissism. It was her own sin nature, that "I-want-to-be-God (and can be)" urge that underlies **every neurotic symptom.**

I must here clarify neurotic symptom. This is in contrast to a symptom of an organic cause. Organic means strictly physical: a brain tumor, lead poisoning, an avitaminosis (loss of vitamins), a post-encephalitic lesion, or an HIV infection of the brain cells, etc. Organic would also include certain kinds of chemical imbalance conditions such as schizophrenia, manic-depressive illness (Bi-polar Disorder), and some kinds of depressive conditions, as well as various others. Electro-chemical misfiring of brain cells impinged upon by an enlarging tumor is not one that the person has any choice about. The agitated aggressive behavior produced therefrom is not subject to a choice. It is physical. It is organic.

A neurotic symptom, on the other hand, is purely psychological. It is one about which the person has a choice. The neurotic agitated aggressive behavior is based on and <u>in</u> choice and could be changed. In that sense, I can determine my mood. That's the basis for the notion that happiness is a choice that is so widely opined about.

Because choices are involved in every neurotic symptom, I present that each one is, in fact, a direct expression or manifestation of the sin nature, in that, there is a maladaptive effort to distort or deny the truth.

Behind her wishful, unconscious, fantasy, magical belief that she has or could seize God's POWER, her projecting it onto her husband so he then can magically provide her with security, and with that she would have attained security in that was where most of her difficulties in functioning as a grown-up had come to be. It is a process of development which can be changed by further clinical therapeutic work.

At this juncture, I moved into further dimensions of relationship in Christian psychiatry. More than seeking to establish Kathy as an independent adult in the world who knows her separation from others, I came to bigger themes and higher states of self-realization than mere secular psychiatry can provide. Kathy and I begin to explore what was the right Christian relationship to God and to the world of His Creation.

As Kathy's understanding developed in the Christian psychiatric setting, she came to see that a dimension of her sense of abandonment—her feeling that no one, including God, was there for her—was something which she, herself, must and could tolerate taking responsibility for. So, she came to know that it was she who abandoned God and not the contrary.

In her childhood, the adversary had used her mother's own sin nature in his efforts to affect his purpose in her life **and get her to turn away from God**. To the extent that she could come to see that God was, *as always*, there for her, she could turn away from the prince of this world and from her pathology and sufferings to find in God the source of her own affirmation, being, separateness, individual personal identity, and self-worth. She could find, then, that He is the only Source of that ultimate Security. He has it all and He will never fail her. We talked, at the appropriate times, about how God in His permissive will and for His Own inscrutable God nature had allowed her mother's behavior.[62] Now, Kathy could exercise her own will in re-embracing Him, knowing He was always loving her, constantly, no matter what the prevailing circumstances.

This Christian psychiatric initiative of mine is not seminary but therapy. I used Christian principles to help the patient find her way back to God and, in that, out of her suffering. "When my father and my mother forsake me, then the Lord will take me up" (Psalm 27:10). Jesus said to those who believe "then are ye my disciples indeed...the Truth shall set you free" (John 8:31-32 KJV). "Peace I leave with you, my peace I give unto you [not as the world giveth, I give unto you.] Let not your heart be troubled, neither let it be afraid" (John 14:27 KJV).

---

[62] Consider: Isaiah 55:8-9 which says in part, "My thoughts are not your thoughts..."

247

One of the greatest things about being a Christian is to know that we are free to **be** guilty—worthy of death, both physical and spiritual—but we don't have to stand constantly in a state of accusation with fear and dreadful expectations. This is only because of the experiential understanding, of God's grace, mercy, love, and forgiveness as **manifested by Jesus on the cross!**

In strengthening Kathy's faith at every possible opportunity, I not only reinforced her mental health, I reinforced her spiritual health as well. We talked over and over about religious mysteries, especially the Resurrection. After all, it is out of Jesus' sacrifice that the Christian finds the guarantee of complete redemption, eternal life, an end to all fears, and their bases in the fear of death. Along with more usual therapeutic interventions, Kathy gained from these the fruits of increasing individuation, greater self-worth, and finally a challenge to her husband to come into therapy himself and to break his part of the pattern. She was able to tell him and to live out a declaration of deep independence: "You are not the source of my being, my worth, my personhood. Nor is my security from you. Even for earthly provision, I can take care of myself, go back to school, and get a job."

In owning her separateness and thereby realigning her relationships, Kathy's life opened to much greater realities and to the whole world through a new relationship with God. She came to know who she is, ultimately and firmly, in her relationship to Christ. He became the Source of her worth. He freed her from fears and earthly dependencies.

So, her case demonstrates with tremendous clarity that the most important relationship in Christian psychiatry is that between person and God. It is further crystalized in the working between both practitioner and patient, with God defined in the great mysteries of the Cross and the Resurrection. These are the summit and basis that comprise all the constituent relationships within Christian psychiatry—body and mind, medicine and spirit, doctor and patient, patient and world, person and God. All we have to do is remember and understand the full implication of what is in the words, "In the beginning God..." (Genesis 1:1a KJV). Everything is by, in, of, and for Him and that He loves you. "We love, because He first loved us" (1 John 4:19, Isaiah 55:8-9; Jeremiah 29:11, Psalm 51:3-17). "**Until** I went into the sanctuary of God; **then understood I** their end" (Psalm 73:17); "My words are health to your flesh" (Proverbs 4:20-22); "Get wisdom and get **understanding**" (Proverbs 4:7).

DR. RYDERISMS

"God ain't stupid and He ain't impractical."

"Every neurotic symptom is a direct expression of the sin nature in that it is a maladaptive effort (it *is* an effort, but one that never achieves its desired, aimed-at purpose) to distort or deny TRUTH."

"Inherent in each of us is the dynamic 'I want what I want, right when I want it, just because I want it, and since it's me that wants it, I have a right to it!' The reality of this is easily demonstrated. Put two toddlers on the floor. Give one 49 toys and the other 1. The one with the 49 will not have played with half of those he has before he wants the 1 the other has. He wants it *all!* Every one of us comes here with that. We do not want to be limited in any way or to any degree. This dynamic is the Sin Nature. The psychological term is Narcissism. (Remember Narcissus? Remember how Lucifer became Satan?)"

"We come to believe when we 'do' a piece of faith, and then we experience God's response. Then, belief becomes understandable, faith intelligible, and we gain peace, comfort and joy even in the face of vulnerability."

"All POWER belongs to God (which leaves *none* for us)!"

"A belief in magic is to believe that one can perform something utterly impossible, but is unconsciously believed to be personally possible as *demonstrated* by *behavior;* fulfilling the wisdom of the old adage 'actions speak louder than words'."

"TRUTH = REALITY: The Truth is that security lies only in the Elohim-God-Power of God in Christ. Truth irresistibly crushes the self-perpetuated lie that man can provide security for himself."

"As far as MY personal salvation goes, Jesus died for me, not for you. As far as YOUR personal salvation goes, Jesus died for you and not for me."

"As Christians, we are free to **be** guilty—worthy of death, both physical and spiritual—but we don't have to stand constantly in a state of accusation with fear and dreadful expectations. This is only because of the experiential understanding, of God's grace, mercy, love, and forgiveness as **manifested by Jesus on the cross!"**

"I can't make you *be* 'weller,' I cannot do it <u>to</u> you. I cannot do it <u>for</u> you. I can only assist you in *your own efforts* to get 'weller'."

"I assume you want to learn more about how you happen to tick the particular way you do so that, hopefully, you can choose to do something differently than what you have been doing."

"The words we choose to say don't come 'out of the air'."

"The evidence of ACCEPTANCE is CHANGE!"

"You can hand me a pound of BRAIN, but you cannot hand me a pound of THOUGHT."

"The brain is not the mind. The mind, however, is a function of the brain, but only as long as whatever the 'I' of 'me' is in this body!"

"There is the actuality of the reality of the immateriality."

"We are all swimming in the same stuff!"

"The Lord ain't just whistling Dixie!"

"The Bible is the most practical book ever written. It is the best 'How To' book going, and the best 'Instruction Book' about how to get along in this stinking world with our stinking selves."

"Practice remembering what God has done!"

BIOGRAPHY

D r. Ryder was born and raised in Alexandria, La. After high school, he enlisted and served in WWII's final Army Cavalry Unit and then began his professional pursuits upon graduating with honors from Louisiana College in 1950. Between 1951 and 1968, Dr. Ryder completed his medical and psychiatric/psychoanalytic training at LSU Medical School in New Orleans, N. La. Hospital & Clinic in Shreveport, Philadelphia Psychiatric Center in Philadelphia, Pa, and Emory University Psychoanalytic Training Institute in Atlanta, Ga.

In 1955, Dr. Ryder returned to his hometown, setting up a general practice of medicine & surgery. He was elected Coroner of Rapides Parish in 1960 until moving his family to Atlanta, Ga., in 1965 to begin his private psychiatric practice. By 1970, having become somewhat disillusioned by the trends of psychiatry and medicine in general, he decided to pursue his entrepreneurial interests more fully. Within a short time his beloved Louisiana lured him to return in 1972 where he continued his private practice in Shreveport until 1989 when he moved to nearby Pineville, La., as Medical Director of River North Treatment Center, which housed a Christian-oriented Rapha ("God Heals") Unit. Thereafter, Dr. Ryder worked as psychiatrist/psychoanalyst as Medical and Clinical Director, Director of Psychiatric Services at several different facilities throughout Central and South Louisiana, including Christian Counseling, VOA, Resource Management Services, Healthy You Social Services, NHS-Human Services, Capitol City Family Health Center, and Stonebridge Behavioral Health.

After several years of God's having been working in his life, and having had his salvation since age 9, and with a powerful moving of the Holy Spirit upon him, Dr. Ryder acknowledged Jesus not only as Savior but as Lord of his life in 1974 and committed his life to Christ. Since that date he committed to and prayerfully studied God's Word. He began teaching Sunday School classes and Bible study groups and in more formal academic situations such as monitoring graduate courses of seminary. Dr. Ryder led and participated in many seminars relating to the problems of everyday living for the Christian. His teaching topics included the "Psychology of Religion," "Sociology from a Christian Perspective," each correlating the secular perspective with the differences involved from a Christian perspective. For more than 45 years practicing "Psychoanalysis and Psychiatric Counseling Founded in Biblical Principles," Dr. Ryder endeavored, through the grace of God, to correlate the valid psychological principles with the spiritual principles of the Bible.

Dr. Ryder has published "Why J. R.?" addressing the problem of the religion of Humanism, its impact on our culture, and the problem of anxiety and depression for Christians. He has other several manuscripts relative to these subjects.

Dr. Ryder was an avid sportsman and athlete, enjoying fishing, hunting, playing cards, football, golf, and even frisbee throughout his life. He and his wife excelled in the exuberant raising of a very large loving and adventurous family of nine, as well as any other who bravely embraced their welcome liveliness. They had nineteen grandchildren and fifteen greats. They were admired by many, but most importantly, were greatly loved and gave huge love.

CPSIA information can be obtained
at www.ICGtesting.com
Printed in the USA
JSHW030821050520
5504JS00003B/3